777

The Spirit of Prague
and other essays

Ivan Klíma was born in 1931 in Prague, where he now lives, and was editor of the journal of the Czech Writer's Union during the Prague Spring. He is the author of many plays, stories and novels including *Waiting for the Dark, Waiting for the Light* and *The Ultimate Intimacy*, which, along with a collection of stories, *My Golden Trades*, are also available from Granta Books. His work, which is now published worldwide, was banned in his country until just a few years ago.

IVAN KLÍMA

The Spirit of Prague

and other essays

TRANSLATED FROM THE CZECH
BY PAUL WILSON

Granta Books
London

Granta Publications, 2/3 Hanover Yard, London N1 8BE

First published in Great Britain by Granta Books 1994
This edition published by Granta Books 1998
Published by arrangement with Brombergs Bokförlag

A CIP catalogue record for this book is
available from the British Library.

5 7 9 10 8 6 4

Printed and bound in Great Britain by Mackays of Chatham PLC

Contents

PREFACE

I SPENT ONLY a few years of my life working as a reporter. I didn't quit the profession voluntarily; the paper I worked for was banned, I was not allowed to write for any other and the papers that were published in my country at the time were the kind I didn't want to write for anyway. Still, the need to express myself on certain issues as quickly and directly as possible remained with me, and so I continued to write—without newspapers or any other means of public dissemination. These pieces were circulated in what was called samizdat, which means they were typed out on ordinary typewriters by friends and, ultimately, by anonymous typists, and in this form passed from reader to reader.

In selecting pieces for this book, I have tried to choose a variety of subjects and genres, partly to persuade the English-speaking reader that the interests of the suppressed writer, far from focusing exclusively on political questions, were similar to the interests of most authors anywhere in the world. Paradoxically, many of the political articles I wrote (some of which I have included) were written after 1989, when I could once again travel freely and when I was asked (mostly abroad) to comment on something about the status of culture or the work of a writer under a totalitarian government.

I wrote the pieces included in this book over a period of fifteen years, though most of them come from the past three years. I have divided them into five sections. The first includes texts of a more personal nature. They reveal something about my life, what motivated me to start writing, and about my relationship to my native city. The second contains some of my *feuilletons*, a genre that has been widely cultivated in the Czech lands and popular with readers. It was *feuilletons* written regularly by Ludvík Vaculík, Václav Havel, Pavel Kohout and many other authors that circulated among Czech readers. The third section contains essays that are more or less political in nature.

I studied literature in university and thus gained (in theory, at least) the right to comment on what my precursors and my colleagues have written; I have therefore included in the fourth part, two general commentaries on the dilemmas facing literature in the modern age. Finally, from my critical and literary historical writings, I have selected a lengthy study of Franz Kafka, which concludes this book.

I

A RATHER UNCONVENTIONAL
CHILDHOOD

I AM TRYING to reach, in memory, to a time before the war began. What was I like then? I think that I inherited my mother's preference for solitude. We lived in a small villa on a road leading out of Prague, north of the industrialized part of the city; my father worked as an engineer in one of the factories. There was another house down the road, and a bar up the road catering to those who did not want to go thirsty into the centre, where they could expect to pay more for drinks. I had no brothers and sisters at the time; my brother was not born until I was seven. A girl about my age lived in our villa, and there was a another boy slightly older than me living in the house down the road. I wasn't close to either of them, and though I did play with other children in the park, I had no real friends, and spent most of my time alone with my toys. Children in those days were not surrounded by toys as they are now, so I can still remember most of mine. What sticks most firmly in my memory is a large curtain made from an old sheet, on which my mother had drawn Walt Disney's three little pigs. Behind this curtain we prepared plays with several stuffed animals for an audience that rarely showed up. From then on, puppet theatre became a passion, and before I grew up I made several of them, one in the concentration camp at Terezín.

Like many children, I was afraid of being alone in the dark, and before going to sleep I would ask for the door to the lighted hallway to be left open. Once in a while, when my parents went out for an evening, I would make a terrible fuss, although they never left me alone in the house; there was usually a maid.

When my mother first took me to school (I was two weeks short of turning six), it was one of the most terrifying experiences of my life. That day they let the parents stay in the classroom, by the door, and I spent the entire first lesson keeping an eye on my mother to make sure she had not abandoned me to the mercies of so many strange children and to the completely unknown woman who was always forcing herself on my attention. Like most children, I did not enjoy going to school (in this sense, the war made my childhood dreams come true, for I was not allowed to go.) But I learned well; I was quiet, and longed for praise though I hardly ever volunteered to answer questions. I was too shy. When I was seven and I had just got used to my classmates, we moved, and I had to get to know a whole new set. The Nazi laws did not permit me to start fourth grade.

Whether it was because I had no friends, or because what followed ruptured my life so completely, I don't know, but in any case I cannot recall a single face or the name of any classmates from that time.

*

My mother and father both came from Jewish families, but my mother's family had adopted the Jewish faith by choice. In the seventeenth century only two religions were permitted in Bohemia: the Jewish and the Roman Catholic. Many Protestant congregations advised their members to adopt Judaism rather than Catholicism, probably reckoning, wrongly, that the ban was temporary and that under the cloak of Judaism they could keep their original faith alive. The temporary state of affairs persisted for more than a century and a half, and over that time, the former Protestants became Jews. I remember that even though my grandfather was a Marxist and a free-thinker, he prayed every Friday evening in a language I couldn't understand. If my grandparents were free-thinkers, my parents rejected not only religion, but their Jewish identity as well. My father believed that technology knew no borders and that therefore he was at home anywhere in the world. My mother thought of herself as a Czech who was proud of her Evangelical ancestors (she even had me baptized, and right after the war I took an active part in the Evangelical youth movement.) I mention this because until the beginning of the war I never heard the word 'Jew', not even as an insult. I did not know the Jewish holidays, and the rituals that punctuated my life were no different from those observed by other children.

At the age of seven, people aren't usually interested in politics, but I can still remember hearing Hitler's name crop up in household conversations and sensing a kind of shapeless monster lurking beneath it. My father used to listen to his speeches on the radio (my parents were fluent in German; I wasn't), and even to me the ranting voice sounded terrifying, though I understood not a single word. Then I learned that, for reasons I could not grasp, we would be moving to England, where my father had the promise of a job. I was worried about moving, but at the same time, I looked forward to the long journey. I also received my first illustrated English textbook and my mother began to learn English with me. My father wanted his mother to come with us, but her visa was slow in coming, and then Hitler arrived and soon after that, the borders closed for the first time in my life— snapped shut like the doors of a cage or, more precisely, like a trap from which there was no escape.

*

In the summer of 1939 we moved for the last time, into Prague itself. Because the building we were to move into was still being completed, my father's aunt Teresa offered us accommodation. Aunt Teresa, the only rich person I knew, owned one of the most beautiful villas in Prague. (After the 1948 revolution the Communists confiscated it; first the prime minister lived there, later the president himself.) Behind the villa was a magnificent garden built into the steep hillside of Troja. Aunt Teresa's daughter and her family also lived in the villa, and thus I came into contact with two of my distant cousins. The younger one, Kitty, was my age, and I formed my first childhood friendship with her. It seems odd now, for the Gestapo were already running the country and almost every week a new anti-Jewish statute was issued, but we children had no idea this was happening. We spent long, happy hours in the gazebo playing cards or mah-jong, gathering fruit or chasing each other around the garden. I could not have known that I was spending my last holiday here for many years, and that three years later Kitty would step into a gas chamber.

My parents managed to hide the true state of affairs from me for another few months, though it is more likely they were hiding it from themselves, or rather, they could not really conceive of what was swiftly to follow.

There was one ban after another. First, I could not leave the city, then I could not go to school, to the theatre, to the movies, to the park or travel in the forward car of the tram.

About that time, Walt Disney's *Snow White and the Seven Dwarfs* came to Prague. The temptation was too powerful to resist; I went and sat through the whole movie in terror of being discovered and cruelly punished. How? I did not know. My experience did not yet include prison, and my imagination failed me. But the fear was all the greater because it had touched the unknown.

In the apartment building we eventually moved to, there were three Jewish families. Lucy, who lived on the ground floor, was slightly older than me, and Tommy, who lived two storeys above, was about a year younger. We befriended each other and played together. At that time, the habits of people living on the outskirts of Prague were like those in small towns and villages. On summer evenings, people would bring chairs outside on to the pavement and sit talking. Though all forms of entertainment were forbidden to us, we were not yet banned from this type of amusement—and we children would hang around close to those from whose midst we would soon be excluded, but who had no objection to our presence. If some of them pitied us they were careful not to show it. Then one September day in 1941, Lucy came running up and told us, in tears, that they were leaving on a transport to Poland. What was a transport? And where was Poland?

Lucy wept and said her farewells to everyone. One of the tenants even gave her a hug. The next day I saw their whole family lugging their suitcases down the street. No one ever saw them alive again. Tommy ended up in a gas chamber a little later.

*

14

The war began when I was two weeks short of my eighth birthday. I soon understood that the outcome of this war was something that immediately concerned my life, and even my survival. When the air-raid sirens went off, I would sit in the basement of our apartment block while the ack-ack pounded. I didn't know what the explosions meant, I only hoped they were English bombs falling, while at the same time I was afraid that the bombs would fall on me and therefore I hoped they weren't bombs at all. I began to take an interest, unusual for my age, in politics and the progress of the war. An enormous map of Europe and the northern shores of Africa hung on the wall of my room. I was not allowed to stick little flags or pins into the map, but every day I followed the shifting of the fronts. Dozens of local names have stuck in my memory and will remain with me till I die, names such as Narvik and Trondheim, Dunkirk, Crete, Tobruk, Banghazi and El Alamein, Orel', Rostov or Voronezh. Many years after the war, when I began to collect old maps, I had an unconscious urge to look up all those old battle sites again—in Greece, in France, in the Ukraine or in the Libyan desert.

I was not allowed to go to school, and gradually, most of the non-Jewish children began to avoid me. The beautiful Marcela, who lived in the neighbouring tenement house and whose father had declared himself a German (he wore a disgustingly flashy swastika in his lapel) began shouting 'Jew!' at me in the street. I didn't know exactly what she meant by it, but I felt ashamed all the same. When the edict came down that I was to wear a six-pointed star on my chest with *jude* written on it, I was even more embarrassed and preferred not to go out at all.

What was I to do at home all day? I read. Of all the books I owned, I was most excited by a prose retelling of Homer's two epics. I read them over and over again, until I knew whole pages by heart. It did not occur to me until years later that, despite the storyteller's bias towards the Greeks, I sided passionately with the Trojans. I admired Hector and I loved Paris for avenging his death: I too lived in a state of siege and I therefore supported those who were themselves surrounded.

At the end of November 1941, my father was summoned to be transported. He didn't go to Poland, but to take part in the preparation of a new camp in the fortified town of Terezín. Several days after that—it was 9 December 1941, exactly half an hour before noon (I remember that Mother was just cooking lunch)—Mother and I received our own summons. There was no mention of my brother, who was three. While others were given three days to prepare, they gave us only two hours.

Mother wept in terror and despair. What would become of my baby brother? While she was crying that she would rather kill herself, I tried to gather my things together and, with the help of neighbours, pack them into a suitcase. Among the essentials were three books: the retelling of Homer, Dickens's *Pickwick Papers* and Verne's *The Children of Captain Grant*. These books were to be my spiritual nourishment for the next three and a half years.

*

That afternoon, I became a real prisoner. I lost my name and was given a number, which of course I remember to this day: L54.

To most people, the incarceration (not to mention the murder) of children is one of the basest and most reprehensible of acts. While this is true, it doesn't say very much about the feelings of children in such a situation. Looking back on my experiences, I would say that I suffered less than the adults around me. Children are more adaptable than adults and especially older people, and they lack the ability (to a considerable extent, at least) to see things in perspective, to comprehend fully their conditions and circumstances. They also perceive space differently—what may seem an unbearably confining prison to an adult, may be a large world to a child—because they have the capacity (as do women, far more than men) to rank the inconsequential over the consequential, in other words, to delight in small things or at least to become absorbed by them, even at a time when they are threatened by death.

I recall the delight I felt when, after months of denial, I was once more sitting in a train, watching the countryside go by. I was actually looking forward to the change. I sensed that it would probably be for the worse, but I didn't think about it. I rejoiced that at the last minute they had brought my little brother to us, and that we would not have to be separated.

They placed us in rooms that belonged to the barracks of

Terezín. Where ten or twelve soldiers had lived, about thirty-five women were to sleep. There was not a stick of furniture in the room. We put the cushions we had brought with us directly on the floor. Because there was not enough space, they had to be placed lengthwise, two to a person. Simple tables were made from suitcases. The women, who mostly came from well-off families and were therefore used to comfort (they had certainly never in their lives before slept on a floor), were devastated by the new conditions. I can imagine how terribly some of them must have suffered: they were afraid for their children, they were plagued by insomnia, disease, discomfort and fear of the future. None of this bothered me at first. On the contrary, my new surroundings were full of adventure. My mood contrasted so sharply with their dejection that it enabled me to overcome my shyness and gain self-confidence. I helped the women carry in their baggage and move from place to place. I felt strong, even capable of offering comfort. They listened to me; some even praised me, and however paradoxical it may sound, my newly won sense of importance in those unfamiliar surroundings made me feel almost happy.

Most of the women adapted incredibly quickly to the new, depressing living conditions. Soon songs and even laughter rang through the rooms. Above all they told many stories, which I listened to with great delight.

Exactly a month after our arrival, the first transport left. No one knew where it was going, but everything had taught us to treat each new step into the unknown as a step towards something worse. The chosen women packed their suitcases again, wept and embraced those who, for the time being, remained behind. I was among those who stayed in the camp.

*

So much has already been recorded about prison life in the concentration camps of Germany and the former Soviet Union that I could only repeat what others have said. For three and a half years, I never saw so much as a morsel of fruit; I never ate a single egg, nor a gram of butter (at the time no one suspected the benefits of such a limited intake of cholesterol), not to mention chocolate or rice, a bun or a piece of carrot. Yet I don't recall that lack of food tormented or preoccupied me most.

Nevertheless, food played a great role in the life of the internees and certainly, beyond the range of what I could see, they bartered and bribed with it in all sorts of ways.

My first love was also connected with food. The story I wrote about her (in the collection called *My First Loves*) is essentially autobiographical. I didn't even change her name, which was Myriam. Roughly a year before the end of the war, they began allotting the children a tiny amount (if I'm not mistaken it was a sixteenth of a litre daily) of skimmed milk. I was thirteen at the time, and the milk was distributed by a girl who might have been two or three years older than me. One day, instead of an eighth of a litre (for my brother and me) she gave me a portion that was at least four times that size. This went on day after day and I could imagine only one reason for this inexplicable generosity: that the girl had fallen in love with me. This circumstance filled me with a happiness as powerful as it was unexpected. The horrors of concentration camp life all but vanished. I was bewildered and distracted, which is perhaps appropriate in one's first love at that age. Myriam seemed to me more beautiful than all the other girls, but I never spoke to her, I merely hung around places where I could at least catch a glimpse of her. At the end of that summer, the Nazis nearly emptied the Terezín camp and sent most of the inmates to Auschwitz. Neither I nor my secret love were among those sent away, but my aunt, who had looked after food supplies in our barracks, was. As soon as she was gone, the extraordinary portions of milk dried up, which abruptly brought me down to earth. Even so, I failed to see the connection between my aunt's departure and the cooling of the young milkmaid's ardour. It was only years later that I learned from my aunt, who survived Auschwitz, that she had ordered the girl to give me more milk. In my story, I tried to hint at this, but I obviously did it so subtly that not a single critic, nor any reader with whom I talked about the story, saw the connection. Perhaps that's as it should be: the mystery of the extra-large portions of milk remains as unsolved for them as it did all those years for me.

I was far more aware of the lack of freedom than I was of the shortage of food. From the camp windows I could see the distant mountains. The fact that I could not go outside the gates of this crowded camp depressed me more than anything else. I remember once in the camp school (the school lasted only a few weeks, and then it was scattered to the winds by the transports) we were asked to write a composition on the subject of our choice. I wrote about the woods in Krč near Prague, and about the park on Petrin Hill; I wrote about trees, not people, because I didn't know much about people. Everyone I knew either shared my fate or was otherwise lost in a world engulfed by war. Trees represented freedom. The forest was associated with a tranquillity that seemed to have survived only in dreams.

My teacher showed her appreciation of the essay by asking me to read it out loud. Perhaps in doing so she helped determine my future calling. But it was more likely that as I was writing the composition, the liberating power that writing can give one was unexpectedly revealed to me. Writing enables you to enter places inaccessible in real life, even the most forbidden spaces. More than that, it enables you to invite your guests along.

*

When you approach fourteen, you occasionally give some thought to what you want to do in life, and if you don't think about it yourself, others will do it for you, for life compels you to decide on a type of school, or employment. In the camp, none of this applied. Like every prisoner, I was powerless to decide anything for myself and I accepted the fact. I was resigned to getting small amounts of miserable food, a piece of inferior soap and a bucket of coal in the winter; such things represented all that one could expect. The future posed only two questions: would I remain here, or would they take me away to places where people are never heard from again? And: when would the war end and would I survive till then? The world in which a person gets an education, works, makes money and buys things with it was so remote as to be unreal.

Life in Terezín was not as strictly ordered as in other concentration camps. No one checked to see whether the barracks were properly cleaned, nor when those who were not required to work got up in the morning, or what they did during the day. Although everyone was constantly treading a thin line between being and non-being, the routine was, at the same time, wearingly monotonous. The day was punctuated by queues: for breakfast, lunch and supper; for the daily ration of bread, coal or margarine; for water, for the washroom or the toilet. The rest of the time we children had to ourselves. Oddly enough, we had a ball, and we would play ordinary games with it, most often volleyball or soccer. Perhaps because I had displayed a certain gift for ball games, I gained some authority among my peers. I was appointed captain in most games, and in this new role my former shyness vanished. I also experienced my first real friendships at this time which, as I later came to understand, were really only prefigurations of the adolescent infatuations that transform every encounter, every casual conversation into an experience of singular importance. All those friendships ended tragically; my friends, boys and girls, went to the gas chamber, all except one, the one I truly loved, Arieh, a son of the chairman of the camp prisoners' self-management committee, who was shot at the age of twelve.

*

Much has been written about the solidarity of prisoners, about how they surrendered their ration of food to someone who badly needed it. Such solidarity certainly existed, and I cannot remember, for instance, that anyone ever stole anything from anyone in our common living space. Yet stealing did go on in the camp at large, stealing of the most important thing of all: food. Even the extra portion of milk I was given over those few weeks was made possible only because someone else got a few drops less. My aunt, who worked in the noodle production plant, occasionally smuggled out a piece of rolled dough next to her body, and that too meant other prisoners had less. The women who worked in the gardening section sometimes spirited out a vegetable, but here they were stealing from our jailers. The punishment for all such thefts was transport, and thus death, yet it went on. I myself managed at times to steal a raw potato or a little coal, and once a friend and I were able to break into the storage room containing the luggage the SS men had stolen from the prisoners, and I got away with a whole suitcase. This successful burglary was such an intense experience that to this day I recall almost everything I found in the suitcase. Even the pattern on a pair of pyjamas.

This kind of thieving can certainly be explained by misery and hunger, but I think that my later experience with the communist regime persuaded me that the causes went deeper than that. The moment a criminal regime disrupts the norms of law, the moment crime is sanctioned, when some people, who are above the law, attempt to deprive others of their dignity and of their basic rights, people's morality is deeply affected. The criminal regime knows this and tries to maintain, through terror, the decent and moral behaviour without which no society, not even a society governed by such a regime, can function. But it has been shown that terror can achieve little where people have lost the incentive to behave morally in the first place.

I filched the suitcase our murderers had stolen from someone else, and I was proud of my act, little appreciating how undignified my pride was.

In later years I came to realize that few things are harder to restore than lost honour, an impaired morality, and perhaps that was why I tried so hard to safeguard these things during the communist regime.

Every society that is founded on dishonesty and tolerates crime as an aspect of normal behaviour, be it only among a handful of the elect, while depriving another group, no matter how small, of its honour and even its right to life, condemns itself to moral degeneration and, ultimately, to complete collapse.

*

The memories of the success of the essays I read out in class remained with me. I wrote several short poems and started to write a novel which, if memory does not mislead me, had nothing to do with my life in the camp, but was about the American West. One of the prisoners who had taught Czech in schools before the war (I have no idea how she found out about my writing) offered to teach me in her free time. She laid out for me the principles of prosody, but theory remained theory, because books of poetry, as of prose, were virtually impossible to come by in Terezín.

Besides writing, I tried my hand at drawing. I was just as untrained in visual art as I was in literature, of course, and I had to work out the techniques of rendering perspective myself, but the fact that I was able to capture the likeness of the room where I lived filled me with satisfaction.

For a long time, I deplored having lost so much time in my education, but when I return to that, after all these years, I would say that compared with the profusion of impressions, information and cultural (and pseudo-cultural) experiences that overwhelm young people today, I truly made the most of what little I encountered. I remember the puppet theatre performed in our barracks, and a concert version of Smetana's *The Bartered Bride*. The presentation of this national opera, which I should properly have seen as a child in the National Theatre in Prague, took place in our prison barracks. There was no orchestra, just the conductor, Mr Schaechter, accompanying the singers on a decrepit old harmonium. The singers, in their best clothes, performed standing on a low podium. I was crammed in with the rest of the audience, which listened in absolute rapture. I saw the tears in many eyes, and felt like crying myself. The experience was utterly intoxicating. Years later, when I went to see a proper production of the opera at the National Theatre, with costumes and an orchestra and chorus, I was disappointed not only by the music, but by the banality of the experience.

*

Hunger, and an enforced sojourn in an enclosed and closely guarded space, certainly made my childhood different from the childhood of most of my contemporaries, but what distinguished it most of all was the constant presence of death. People died in the room where I lived. They died by the dozens. Corpse carriers marched through my childhood, funeral wagons piled high with wooden boxes of unplaned, unpainted wood, wagons pushed and pulled by people, many of whom soon ended up on those wagons themselves. Every day, by the gates, I read long lists of those who had not lived to see the morning. The constant threat of the transports hung over us, and even though I knew nothing of the gas chambers, they seemed to carry people into a bottomless chasm. Anyone who ended up on one of them vanished and was never heard from again. In the final days of the war, when they cleared out the camps in Poland and eastern Germany and brought the inmates to Terezín, I saw each day wagons piled with wretched corpses.

From the sunken, sallow faces, stone-still eyes often stared out at me, eyes that had had no one to close them. Stiffened arms and legs, and bare scalps jutted towards the skies.

When you live with death all around you, you must, consciously or unconsciously, develop a kind of resolution. The knowledge that you can be murdered tomorrow evokes a longing to live intensively; the knowledge that the person you are talking to can be murdered tomorrow, someone you may be fond of, leads to the fear of intimacy. You build in yourself a kind of wall behind which you conceal what is fragile in yourself: your deepest feelings, your relationship to other people, especially to those closest to you. This is the only way to bear the repeated, despairing and inevitable partings.

If you construct such an inner wall when you are still a child, you must then spend the rest of your life tearing it down, and the question is, can you ever manage to destroy it completely?

*

With death walked fear. I knew that I was at the mercy of a force that had no feeling, a force that could do anything it wanted. I knew I could be included at any time in the transport and taken away to places from which there was no return. I knew that at any moment, a man in a greyish-green uniform with a human skull on his cap could appear before me and beat or kill me.

An adult may accept fear and submit to it, or close himself to it. But a child has no real choice in the matter. A child can only cling desperately to a blind faith in the world in which it has grown up, that is, a fairy-tale world in which the forces of good triumph in a never-ending battle with the forces of evil; where witches are outwitted and dragons beheaded. It may seem paradoxical to talk of a fairy-tale world in the context of a concentration camp, but it was not just my peers and I who escaped into that world; the adults, whose powerlessness did not differ very much from ours, did so as well. Their world, like ours, was polarized into a primordial struggle between good and evil. It was a struggle in which our very lives were decided, and it took place somewhere in the distance, beyond our capacity to influence or affect it. Nevertheless—and I remember this very well—almost everyone believed good would prevail and the war would soon be over. This faith helped them to sustain themselves and survive the humiliations, the anxiety, the disease and the hunger.

But the world, of course, is not a fairy-tale world, least of all at that time and in those places, and that sustaining faith proved hollow for most of the people around me. I, however, survived; I lived to see the end of it. For me, the forces of good, embodied chiefly in the Red Army, did in fact triumph and, like many who survived the war, it took me some time to understand fully that often it is not the forces of good and evil that do battle with each other, but merely two different evils, who compete with each other for control of the world.

*

However, in prison camp conditions, a black-and-white vision of the world is reinforced by powerful emotional experiences. I longed for one moment so intensely that it seemed almost unreal: the moment of liberation.

Many people in our part of the world suffer from the feeling that their lives lack excitement, a deeper happiness, and they try to find what they lack through drugs or mysticism. Few realize that a profound experience of happiness is impossible without an equally profound experience of deprivation.

To this day I remember every detail of the day when I stood by the razed prison fence, which I had once understood I would never be allowed to cross, and watched as endless columns of Red Army soldiers, tired horses, exhausted people, dirty tanks, cars and cannon, all filed by, and for the first time I saw a portrait of Marshal Stalin, a man whose name I long afterwards associated with that moment, and I sobbed uncontrollably at the knowledge that I was free. As I watched, a German civilian was beaten to death, and a tank ran over a prisoner who too greedily flung himself on a pack of cigarettes someone had tossed on the ground, but none of this could spoil my mood or bring me down from the heights of my bliss. Years later, when I remembered my childhood and what had happened to me, an almost blasphemous thought occurred: that all those years of deprivation were worth that single, supreme sensation of freedom.

In a similar way, extraordinary moments of bliss purchased by long years of suffering often determine the lives not just of individuals, but of whole nations. This is not necessarily something positive. On the contrary, the sensation of supreme happiness is the most transient of feelings, yet it can colour our judgement for a long time afterwards, despite the inevitable sobering up to follow, which causes deep frustration.

I mentioned the feeling of powerlessness I shared with the adults. That was one of the strongest experiences of my childhood: the impotence of those around me in the face of the terrible destiny we were forced to march towards.

Endless lines of ignominiously branded and doomed people accompanied by a handful of armed men stretch through my childhood. The image of those lines, whose length can be calculated in kilometres, but the sum of whose despair is beyond measure, has stayed with me all my life and often determines the circle of ideas and themes that attract me.

*

Sometimes, when I think about my life and work, it occurs to me that for a writer, any experience, even the most drastic, is useful, should he survive it. By that I don't just mean that the most horrific experiences generally make for better storytelling than what routine life offers. Powerful and extreme experiences, when we stand on the very dividing line between life and death, or when, on the contrary, we know the bliss of sudden salvation, usually form us more clearly than anything else in life. But extreme experiences can unbalance our judgement. Seen from a point of disjunction, from a borderline, the world usually appears to us as other than we normally perceive it. Questions of guilt and punishment, of freedom and oppression, of rights and lawlessness, of love and hate, of vengeance and forgiveness, seem quite simple, particularly in the eyes of a young person who has no other experience of life.

I recall how obsessed I was after the war with the idea of vengeance. Every day, I listened breathlessly to live broadcasts of the many trials that took place at the time, with Czech collaborators as well as with the most prominent Nazis. I rejoiced in accounts of the executions of those condemned in the main trial in Nuremberg. I don't think I was very different from most of my contemporaries in this, but it wasn't long before I suddenly realized what the roots of those feelings really were, and that led me to reconsider my too simple judgements.

The realization I came to, and that I attempted to express in my prose was this: the extraordinary experiences that we have gone through in this century as individuals and as groups can make us go badly astray. Moved by the desire to draw conclusions from our bitter experience, we are led to make fatal mistakes which, instead of bringing us closer to the state of freedom and justice we wish to achieve, take us in the opposite direction. In themselves, extreme experiences do not open the way to wisdom. We can only achieve that if we are able to judge our experiences from a distance.

*

The events of childhood no doubt influence a person for the rest of his life. The relationship between them and what follows, however, is generally far from direct. I know people somewhat older than I was at the time who are permanently possessed by a feeling of paranoia, the expectation that what happened to them then can happen again at any time. In my case, the experience had an opposite effect. It seemed to me that what I had gone through could never be repeated, and the fact that I had survived filled me with an expectation, difficult to justify rationally, that I would happily survive everything I would ever encounter in life again. My wartime experience certainly helped me to survive, with a kind of distance, the years of persecution that dominated my adulthood.

If wartime experiences awakened in some people a longing for vengeance, it also hardened them for life towards anyone they considered an enemy, or even a potential opponent. Put simply, as victims of one kind of fanaticism, they often succumbed to fanaticism of an opposite kind.

With a certain distance, I have come to the conclusion that fanaticism of any kind is a psychological precondition, a precursor, of violence and terror, that there is no idea in the world good enough to justify a fanatical attempt to implement it. The only hope for the salvation of the world in our time is tolerance. On the other hand, those helpless, desperate multitudes driven, be it 'merely' into camps surrounded by wire and machine-gun towers, or directly into gas chambers or before firing squads, warn us that tolerance has its limitations. There is no disputing the fact that Hitler and his cronies (just as Lenin and his gang of revolutionaries) made no secret of their destructive intentions to limit the freedom of entire large groups of people, nor did they make any secret of their fanatical determination to achieve their ends regardless of the cost. If they had not encountered unpardonable indifference, hesitation and weakness, they might have been restrained. Tolerance must never mean tolerance of intolerance, tolerance of those who are prepared to limit the freedom or even the right to life, of anyone else, though it be justified by the most noble of ends.

I know that these are essentially simple principles, but over the years I have often been persuaded that it is precisely these truisms that are the hardest to uphold. Over and over again, we watch helplessly as multitudes march towards a fate prepared for them by some new mutation of fanaticism, one that we are, for mostly selfish reasons, prepared to tolerate, or at least publicly declare our helplessness to do anything about. Over and over again, we miss the moment when it might have been possible to end the violence without a great deal of bloodshed. Experience warns me that if we don't learn from catastrophes and if we don't accept these simple principles, the moment when we might have done something to decide the fate of mankind will pass us by.

HOW I BEGAN

I AM A native of Prague. I was born in the middle of the Great Depression and on the eve of a political crisis that shook the world. I mention the Depression not because it directly affected our family, but because it influenced the thinking of part of my parents' generation. Like many of their contemporaries, my parents stopped believing in democracy. To them, society seemed sick and in need of radical transformation. My father was a top specialist in his field—the construction of electrical machines, mainly commutators and electric welders. He also played the piano and knew Latin and six living languages. But by nature he was a technologist. He was certain that there were no limits to human reason and skill, that society had to be organized and planned according to precise blueprints. Thus, in his youth, he succumbed to the delusion that a socialist utopia was possible.

For the first few years of my life I was generally happy. We lived in a modest villa on a hillside overlooking a complex of factories belonging to the ČKD company where my father worked. There was a bar on one side, and a house on the other, and then nothing but wood lots and meadows. A short distance below us was a railway track and I used to love watching the locomotives as they laboured up the hill, spewing out sparks and columns of smoke. Several families lived in our house. Once, when I was playing with a girl of about my age, she bit my hand, perhaps to express her love. A hunting dog lived there as well, and though I loved him, he clearly did not return my affection; at any rate, he never bit me.

How I Began

The Depression gave way to recovery, and my father bought a small car that we called Baby. There weren't many automobiles around in those days. Most of the vehicles that stopped in front of the bar were still pulled by horses. Below us were dozens of belching smokestacks (there were other factories besides the ČKD works) and there was an airport nearby; aircraft were constantly droning overhead.

I was still too young to understand anything of the gathering political crisis. The first event from the larger world around me that I can remember was the death of President Masaryk. It happened on my sixth birthday. My mother had prepared my favourite treat, cookies made of flour, sugar and egg yolks that we called 'little wreaths'. She brought them to the table, but instead of smiling at me, she was crying. Some time later our school principal came round to check our coloured pencils. Anyone who had Hardtmuth brand pencils had to stop using them, the principal said, because they were made in Germany. I had just got a new set and didn't understand (and I still don't to this day) why these pencils couldn't be used to serve their purpose. I was outraged by the ban. It was utterly insignificant compared with the outrages that were to come, but the memory is still vivid precisely because it was of a dimension that I was able to grasp.

My parents were atheists, and though their parents still embraced Judaism, they themselves did not feel Jewish. Both came from poor families and had to support themselves at school by giving private lessons, and perhaps this was why, although they never joined the party, both sympathized with the Communists.

Because my father took an interest in politics, he foresaw, correctly as it turned out, what would happen to us if Hitler's Germany were to swallow Czechoslovakia. He found a job in an electrotechnical plant in Liverpool, and all of us (by this time my brother had been born) except his mother got visas to England. But he didn't want to leave her behind, so we ended up not going. The only souvenir of this aborted journey is a large trunk that to this day stands in my mother's flat.

I began to write in the Terezín concentration camp: a poem on suicide and three short sketches about Prague. I wrote them as composition exercises in a makeshift school I attended in Terezín over a period of about two months. It was my only formal schooling during the five years of war. Later, this gave me an advantage over my fellow students: they had to forget what they had been taught; I did not.

My schooling was altogether rather eccentric. There were no new textbooks after the war and so, with great effort, we hunted down old pre-war ones. Not quite three years later, in February 1948, the Communists seized power and not only did they ban all former textbooks, old or new, they also repudiated most of what had once passed for learning.

I was accepted as a student at the philological department of the Charles University at the beginning of 1952. At that time, Stalinist ideology ruled all areas of intellectual life. The intellectual independence of every institution of higher learning, including my famous university, was destroyed. The humanities departments, of course, were the most profoundly affected, and I was studying literature and a branch of it called literary science, although it should more properly have been called 'literary pseudo-science'. I learned that the only permissible method in art was socialist realism. I also learned that 'the name of Sartre has become, for the world's cultural community, a symbol of decay and moral degeneration, a prototype of the mire into which bourgeois pseudo-culture has sunk.' I learned that Steinbeck's obscurantism had practically reached the level of a mental illness, whereas Faulkner's hero represented 'organized training in murder'. The 'American pornographer Henry Miller' was also alleged to have recommended that the reader transform himself into a brutal murderer. For many of our lecturers, Stalin's work on linguistics became the bible.

The worst of it was that all these books, the dregs of western culture, were inaccessible: they had vanished from the libraries and bookshops. I soon understood that I had to do what my fellow students were doing: forget what we were being taught, or use it as a guide to self-education. The works and authors my teachers most condemned belonged among the best of world literature.

Still, my years of study were not wasted. In my second year, I decided that I would complete my studies with a thesis on Karel Čapek, and I began the preliminary research. Čapek had embodied the democratic spirit of the First Republic. He was a proponent of Anglo-American pragmatism, a personal friend of Masaryk, a long-time chairman of the Czech PEN club and a humanist in his writing. In everything he did, he opposed totalitarian ideologies and systems, which means he was one of the chief opponents of Nazism and fascism. This was precisely what confused the communist ideologists after 1948. First they banned Čapek's works, then they granted clemency to the 'anti-fascist' part of him. My dissertation was called *Karel Čapek's Struggle Against Fascism*, but it dealt with Čapek's life, work and philosophy. Thanks to Čapek I was able to spend time among the literary legacy of the First Republic. With harsh ideological indoctrination going on all around me, I was able to read magazines and newspapers in whose pages the great minds of the inter-war period spoke freely to me.

In 1953 they arrested my father. Fortunately Stalin had just died, and after more than a year in solitary confinement, my father was sentenced to eighteen months rather than the expected ten to fifteen years. Nevertheless, the experience of a communist prison opened his eyes and the eyes of everyone in our left-thinking family.

After I returned from the Nazi concentration camp, I never had doubts about my future profession. I wanted to write. I had an unusual amount of experience for my age, but knew nothing about literature, either in theory or in practice. In Terezín, books were one of the things that were forbidden. Still, I managed to bring a retelling of Homer, Dickens's *Pickwick Papers* and Verne's *The Children of Captain Grant* with me, and for a long time I knew the latter two almost by heart. But they were not exactly a rich source of reading matter for an aspiring author. After the war I discovered the beauty and the delight of reading, but when I had read a few books I was overcome by a strange impatience. Real delight came to me not so much from reading as from writing. Yet like many who are just starting to write, I set no store by my own experience, and plunged into the dream-filled world of my imagination. I began to write novels. At a time when I was too bashful to speak to young women, I began to compose a thick romantic novel. It was an epic I called *Great Heart*, but all that remains of it—and of my next novel, *One of Thousands*, three plays and many short stories—are two school exercise books that survived a wave of self-criticism only because they ended up by mistake among some older papers filled with geography notes and Latin translations. One of them contains the opening of the romantic epic mentioned above. On the first page, along with the title and the all-important author's name, I found this note: 'The first volume contains Part One: pp1–74, December 1947; Part Two: 75–280; Part Three: 281–380, January–May.' I can no longer say whether the page numbers represent pages I actually wrote, but the dates correspond to the period of my first, entirely platonic love for a classmate who had a limp. What others dealt with in three poems, I poured into a novel that absorbed all the time that others might have used to fulfil their romantic ambitions.

I can still remember coming home from school every afternoon and sitting down to write. All day I looked forward to that moment, when I could tell my story, the noble story of a grand passion of which I was the sole and unlimited creator and master. I have never since felt such pleasure and delight in the act of creation as I did then, when I was cobbling together my first (and from a literary point of view, dismal) story about the great love of a student, Jiří, for the nubile, gentle, but handicapped Lenka. I invented many heart-rending scenes of misunderstanding, and put obstacles (always happily overcome) in their way only so that I could then describe wonderful reunions. When I got this far I was happy. I had written the great love story unfolding in my imagination, and through it, had felt what I had not experienced in reality. I was choked with the enormous emotions of my heroes. Reading these scenes years later, I saw that they contained none of the powerful feelings that made me tremble at the time. All that remained was a little sentimentality, and some borrowed literary banalities. I learned that the results bear no relation to what the author is feeling or going through at the time of writing. Storytelling has its own kind of law and order, which can be in conflict with the emotional order of the storyteller. The tragedy of compulsive writers and bad authors is that they often put everything they have into their work but the work itself bears no trace of this. Writing was, after all, rather more complicated than it first seemed to me. This is fortunate. If it were not so, the world would have many more writers than it does today, and would drown in an avalanche of printed paper. Which may well be one of the ends that awaits it.

LITERATURE AND MEMORY

I HAVE OFTEN been asked what I am writing, but no one has ever asked me why I write. Nor have I ever been questioned about the most fundamental thing of all: what literature means to me, and what I understand by that term. People may have been reluctant to ask my reasons for writing: perhaps they thought it might embarrass me. They probably refrained from asking the second question, about literature, because they considered it pointless.

In fact the answer is by no means self-evident.

It used to be that everything written was considered literature. Livy, Tacitus, as well as Cicero and Virgil, were simply literary creators. We call the Bible 'the Book of Books', and in it we find mythical tales alongside ritualistic prescriptions, historical chronicles, collections of proverbs, codices of laws and love poetry. Many ancient and medieval works on the subject of law, medicine, geography or mathematics were written in verse. In them, fantasy often outweighed fact, and today we read them as literature rather than for their scientific merit. It was only recently that we began to think of technical, specialist writing as separate from literature. And how are we to classify the flood of trash that washes over readers every day? Where is the precise borderline between what is literature and what is not? Of course there are many demarcation lines and definitions. Most of them deal with the formal or the aesthetic qualities of the work. The attempt to define literature formally reached a peak in structuralistic theories and definitions, which may have been able to distinguish scientific works from works of art, but lost sight of the content and, with it, a number of essential qualities that often separate genuine art from mere entertainment. Moreover, structuralists have little interest in the impact of the work on society. I am not raising this question to draw attention to a theoretical problem, but because, as a writer, I would like to define as precisely as I can the subject and the meaning of the activity I engage in.

Two hundred years ago, the founder of German classical philosophy, Immanuel Kant, asked a similar question in his *Critique of Judgement*. He was trying to distinguish between science and art (art is creation in a condition of freedom) and then between art and craft (which, in a brilliant distinction, he defined as art for profit). Kant too, of course, was aware of the necessity of aesthetic qualities in a work, as well as of content, which must be a subject of contemplation, but what is worth noticing is that he pays close attention to the role of the creator, or, in his terminology, the genius, without whom a true work of art cannot come into being. I don't wish to analyse Kant's definition of the phenomenon of the creator or his activity, but his discovery that it is impossible to come to any precise understanding of the nature of an artistic (and therefore literary) work without considering the qualities of its creator, his thinking and his motivation is essential.

This brings me back to the question I raised at the beginning: why do I write? It is a question seldom asked of writers, yet the answer tells us a great deal. Here, for instance, is what the Greek writer Nikos Kazantzakis says about what motivates him: 'Inside us there is layer upon layer of darkness—raucous voices, hairy, hungering beasts. Does nothing die, then? Can nothing die in this world? The primordial hunger, thirst and tribulation, all nights and moons before the coming of man, will continue to live and hunger with us, thirst and be tormented with us as long as we live. I was terror-stricken to hear the fearful burden I carry in my entrails begin to bellow. Would I never be saved? . . . I am the latest and most beloved grandchild, after all; aside from me they (my ancestors) have no hope or refuge. Whatever remains for them to avenge, enjoy or suffer, only through me can they do this. If I perish, they perish with me . . . ' And this passionate confession ends with an equally passionate formulation of the writer's mission: ' . . . I knew my true face and my sole duty: to work this face with as much patience, love and skill as I could manage. To "work" it? What did that mean? It meant to turn this flame into light, so that Charon would find nothing of me to take. For this was my greatest ambition: to leave nothing for death to take—nothing but a few bones.' [Nikos Kazantzakis, *Report to Greco*, p26, Bruno Cassirer, Oxford, 1965.]

When I first read this passage, I was astonished at how close Kazantzakis had come to expressing my own answer to the questions of why I write and what I expect of my writing. I remember how I felt in the final days of the war: I had spent most of it in a concentration camp; I had survived while almost everyone around me—my contemporaries as well as people of my parents' and my grandparents' generations—had perished. At the time I was overwhelmed by a similar feeling of having been given a task or a mission: to become their voice, their cry of protest against a death that had erased their lives from the world. It was probably this feeling that drove me to write, though I certainly don't want to underplay the factor of my excitement at the very act of writing, of creating stories and looking for the best way of conveying to others what I wished to say.

The feeling that it was up to me to become the voice of others returned to me, in various forms, at other times. In periods of unfreedom, when we were bombarded with lies, when it seemed that everything real, everything that aimed higher than man, did not in fact exist and was condemned to nothingness and forgetting—at times like this, one wrote to overcome this confusion. One wrote to defy death, which assumed so many different forms, each of which always made reality, human destiny, suffering, defiance and truthfulness vanish under its hand. In one way or another, this feeling was shared by most writers who worked, or even merely lived for some time, in unfree conditions. We wrote to preserve the memory of a reality that seemed to be sinking irrevocably into an imposed and enforced forgetting. To quote from Milan Kundera's *The Book of Laughter and Forgetting*, 'Nations are destroyed by first robbing them of their memory. Their books are destroyed, their learning, their history. And then someone else writes different books, gives them a different kind of learning and invents a different history.' In the same book Kundera coined a phrase that inspired me: he called the president that embodied the communist system 'the President of Forgetting'. A nation led by the President of Forgetting is heading towards death. And what applies to nations also applies to individuals, to each of us. If we lose our memory, we lose ourselves. Forgetting is one of the symptoms of death. Without memory we cease to be human beings.

The struggle to transcend our own death is quintessentially human. The feeling that death should not be the end of everything is one of the basic existential feelings. By resisting death, we resist forgetting, and vice versa: by resisting forgetting, we resist death. One form this resistance can take, to come back to the passionate confession of Kazantzakis, is the act of creation. Consciously or unconsciously, this conviction must be present in the creator's mind: because I create, I resist death. *Exegi monumentum aere perennius.* This is why we cannot ignore the question of why we write, why we create, if we contemplate the meaning and value and authenticity of creation.

After the war was over, I did not conclude from the fact of my survival that it was my duty to write realistic works about the war and the camps, and in fact I wrote very little about all that. Memory is not expressed only through a dutiful recording of a certain experience; it is, rather, a responsibility that flows from an awareness of a continuity with everything that went before, with all those who came before, that is, a responsibility for what must not be forgotten if we are to avoid ending up in a vacuum. The sense of acceleration our civilization is experiencing, the profusion of information that surrounds us with its hum, brings with it the danger that we will end up in this emptiness, that we will tear ourselves loose from our roots and fall into timelessness, nothingness. The same danger threatens literature, and all of art. At a certain moment in modern history, it seemed to many that memory and tradition were merely a burden that had to be cast off. The social catastrophes that befell humanity in our century were assisted by an art that worshipped originality, change, irresponsibility, avant-gardism, that ridiculed all former traditions and sneered at the consumer, the audience in the gallery and the theatre, that took a smug delight in shocking the reader instead of responding to the questions that tormented him. It doesn't matter that the totalitarian regimes that came into being about this time rejected avant-garde literature as degenerate; the essential thing was that they assumed the avant-garde's dismissive attitude to tradition and traditional values, to the genuine memory of humanity, and then tried to force upon literature a counterfeit memory and false values.

Every few seconds a new book sees the light of day. Most of them will just be a part of the hum that makes us hard of hearing. Even the book is becoming an instrument of forgetting. A truly literary work comes into being as its creator's cry of protest against the forgetting that looms over him, over his predecessors and his contemporaries alike, and over his time, and the language he speaks. A literary work is something that defies death.

Delivered at a conference in Lahti, Finland, 1990

THE SPIRIT OF PRAGUE

I HAVE TRAVELLED widely in the past couple of years. I have
visited many cities and seen a lot of cathedrals, museums,
galleries, gardens and palaces. It has left me with a strange
mixture of impressions, and a feeling of uncertainty about
where I saw what. The uncertainty is not the result of a bad
memory; it was because I seldom had time to enter into any
relationship with those cities. A city is like a person: if we don't
establish a genuine relationship with it, it remains a name, an
external form that soon fades from our minds. To create this
relationship, we must be able to observe the city and understand its peculiar personality, its 'I', its spirit, its identity, the
circumstances of its life as they evolved through space and time.

Many studies and essays have been written about the spirit
of Prague. Books have come out with titles like *Magic Prague*
or *Prague, the Mystical City*. The interesting thing is that these
books were written by foreigners. The finest and best informed
book about Prague I have ever read was written by an Italian,
A. M. Ripellino; others have been written by Prague Germans or
Jews who, for the most part, had to emigrate from
Czechoslovakia to escape the Nazis. Their portraits of Prague, it
would seem, have dominated the imaginations of many visitors
to my native city. It is the portrait of a mysterious and exciting
city that has inspired people's creativity by its ambience, by the
remarkable and stimulating blend of three cultures that lived
side by side for decades, even centuries: the Czech, German
and Jewish cultures. '*Ich bin hinternational*,' punned the
German-speaking Prague native Johannes Urzidil. To him, the

milieu of Prague had a fairy-tale beauty precisely because you could live here 'beyond nationality', because conflicts of nationality cancelled each other out and gave birth to a kind of immaterial, indefinable, mysterious world, a space that could be considered neither Czech, nor German, nor Jewish, nor even Austrian. Urzidil, like many of his contemporaries, drew his picture of Prague and its streets teeming with strolling city-dwellers, but he also depicted a Prague of picturesque empty lanes, nightclubs, open-air stages, theatres and cabarets, tiny shops, small cafés and, above all, beer halls and taverns, student societies and literary salons, and of course brothels and the colourful metropolitan underworld. Of course, this portrait was dominated by the experience of his generation, but also by the remarkable number of great spirits who lived here at the turn of the century. Think only of the composers Dvořák and Smetana, the writers Hašek, Kafka, Rilke, Werfel, Urzidil, Brod, and the politician Masaryk. The Czech and German theatres were enlivened by a generation of great actors and singers; Albert Einstein lectured at the German University; and the Czech Charles University, after a long, arid period, could pride itself on a great many scholars with worldwide reputations in their field. Such an agglomeration of brilliant creative spirits cannot, of course, be explained by external circumstances, for such circumstances contribute only to a place in which brilliance can express itself. But in its dying years, the Austrian empire did provide sufficient room for free creation, and that spirit, as if in anticipation of the impending catastrophe, permeated the life of the city.

But to my mind it was not freedom that most influenced the shape and the spirit of Prague, it was the unfreedom, the life of servitude, the many ignominious defeats and cruel military occupations. Prague as it was at the turn of the century no longer exists, and those who might have remembered that period are no longer alive. Jews murdered, Germans banished, many great personalities driven out and scattered across the world, small shops and cafés closed: this was the heritage Prague brought to the new *fin de siècle*.

Of course the spirit that prevailed at the end of the last century and the beginning of this one no longer exists anywhere in the world. It's just that elsewhere, the transition was less drastic and less obvious. But what kind of spirit prevails in the present city?

•

Prague was chosen as a capital city by the Přemyslid dynasty. The territory it ruled from here was not large, but its geographical position in the middle of Europe destined it to be a place where many foreign interests would clash. Soon after the beginning of recorded history, the Czechs were joined by others: first by Jews, and, in the thirteenth century, by Germans. They all lived under a common ruler in a land for which the German language had a special word that did not exist in Czech: 'Boehmen'. Unlike later interpretations influenced by the nationalisms of the nineteenth and twentieth centuries, the original sources tell us that for the most part the Czechs and the German colonists got along well together, whether they lived in the border regions or right in the capital city. The lives of the Jews were more precarious, and the hatemongers who from time to time vented their rage against them sometimes spoke Czech and sometimes German. Otherwise, all those who lived in the land suffered equally during plagues and wartime.

There was scarcely a war in Europe that did not affect the Czech state. Prague was frequently besieged and occupied, yet despite—or perhaps because of—this, the city preferred to negotiate and even capitulate rather than fight back. Such policies (often criticized) have enabled it to survive, though not without losses.

In 1620, when the Czech aristocracy squandered its independence in an unsuccessful uprising against the Habsburg dynasty, the country lost even the limited freedom it had enjoyed until then. Prague was plundered not only by the occupying forces but also by those who ruled over it. Almost nothing is left of the magnificent art collections assembled under Rudolf II, although at the beginning of the seventeenth century they had been among the most valuable and extensive in the world. Paintings were carted away to Vienna after Rudolf's death, and shortly after that many were taken as booty by the Swedes (one of the many nations that have conquered Prague). What was left was gradually removed to Vienna by subsequent Habsburg rulers.

But the material damage was only part of the misfortune that befell the city. The Protestant clergymen were exiled from the land, and most of the gentry left too. Government, education and even the custody of people's souls fell into the hands of foreigners. Once the seat of kings and a centre of humanistic scholarship, Prague became a holiday resort for the court of Vienna. The first European city to lead the resistance to the Catholic Church was Catholicized as quickly as possible, by force when necessary.

One of the epithets most frequently applied to Prague is the expression 'the city of a hundred spires'. Few people realize that many of its steeples and baroque cathedrals were built in this period of Catholicization, a time that for many is associated with violence, enforced exile, a loss of homeland or at least a loss of one's original religion.

At the same time, however, it cannot be claimed that the city experienced only losses. New preachers of the faith came and built new churches, new rulers commissioned new palaces for themselves, and all this helped create a livelihood for the burghers and the common people of Prague. It was during this period that the most admired palaces and gardens were designed and erected by the best architects of European Baroque.

And yet something had been broken. Something of that defeat affected the spirit of the city permanently, for except for several short periods, that defeat, that loss of freedom, that subjugation to foreign rulers were never undone. Instead, in ever-quickening succession, came new defeats and new losses. Yet it is part of the mystery of this city that it was able to extract something positive from even so unpropitious a fate.

One of the most striking features of Prague is its lack of ostentation. Franz Kafka (like many other intellectuals) used to complain that everything in Prague was small and cramped. He almost certainly meant the circumstances of life, but it is also true of the city itself, of its physical dimensions. Prague is one of the few big cities where you will not find a single tall building or triumphal arch in the centre, and where even many of the palaces, though magnificent inside, put on an inconspicuous and plain face, almost like military barracks, and seem to be trying to look smaller than they really are. At the end of the last century, the people of Prague built a sort of copy of the Eiffel Tower, but they reduced it to a fifth of its original size. In the period between the two world wars, they built dozens of schools, gymnasiums, hospitals, but they did not build a grandiose parliament like the ones in London, Budapest, or Vienna. In 1955 the Communists erected a gigantic monument to the Soviet dictator Josef Stalin; seven years later, they destroyed it again themselves.

What might have been felt as pettiness or provinciality at the beginning of the century, we perceive today rather as a human dimension, miraculously preserved.

A sense of proportion permeated the life of people as well. Czech life does not go in for a great deal of ostentation, for Barnum & Bailey-sized ads, fireworks, dazzling society balls, casinos or grand military parades. It tends rather towards markets, seasonal festivals and simple dances. The showiest celebration used to be the Sokol gymnastic competitions, held in what at the time was the largest sports stadium in the world (it was built on the outskirts of the city so that its vastness would not be disruptive). Such events brought together tens of thousands of gymnasts who would perform synchronized routines in front of audiences approaching 200,000. But even events like this were more an expression of moderation and disciplined enthusiasm than of a longing to amaze the world.

*

A history that unfolds peacefully seems to flow somewhere beyond people's awareness, but a history full of uprisings and reversals, occupations, liberations, betrayals and new occupations, enters the life of people and cities as a burden, as a constant reminder of life's uncertainties. Prague does not have many public monuments or memorials, but it does have many buildings in which innocent people were imprisoned, tortured or executed, and they were usually the best people in the country. It is part of Prague's restraint that it does not display these wounds, as though it wished to forget about them as quickly as possible. That is why they are always tearing down monuments to those who symbolized the most recent past (monuments to the emperors and to the first, second and now even the fourth president, monuments raised to honour conquerors). Streets are also constantly being renamed. Some have had five name changes this century alone. Strangers can walk the streets oblivious to this; a visitor who knows an area can be confused by it and wonder if he has gone astray. Street signs with new names testify to an attempt to purge the city of something it cannot be purged of—its own past, its own history, a history that seems too great a burden to bear.

For a person to bear the burden of his own destiny, and a nation the burden of its own history, patience and perseverance are necessary. A city, too, must have these qualities. In Czech, as in many other languages, the word for patience (*trpělivost*) has the same root as the verb to suffer (*trpět*). This city, apparently spared the ravages of war, has had to bear greater suffering than many cities directly affected by belligerent action. Unlike foreigners, whose journey usually takes them only to places accessible to tourists, I have been able to enter old buildings and some former palaces and see how self-appointed, barbaric caretakers have allowed ceilings to collapse or have run new walls through magnificent salons and transformed them into company canteens or offices. I have seen terraced gardens that were among the most beautiful in Europe eaten away by the damp; untended flower-beds left to die; churches turned into warehouses and finally into spaces unsuitable even for storage. If Prague is still standing, and has not yet lost its allure or its beauty, it is because its very stones, like its people, have expressed their patient perseverance.

•

I have often wondered which place in Prague could be considered its symbolic centre. The Castle? The Old Town Square? Wenceslas Square? The Castle, although it is the most common image on postcards and is most often rendered by artists, symbolizes something different for me. Wenceslas Square, which was a market-place until the nineteenth century, lacks an intimate historical connection with the fate of the city. And the Old Town Square? It, without doubt, embodies the burden of Czech history. For almost four centuries it has been marked by the ignominious public execution in 1621 of twenty-seven Czech noblemen, burghers and spiritual leaders. It has become a symbol of humiliation, of human duplicity and the fickle adaptability of the Prague people. Time and time again, celebrations have been held on this spot to honour the current rulers, whether loved or (more commonly) not, and sufficient people have always been found to come and pay homage, either out of interest or because they were driven by fear.

For me, the material and spiritual centre of the city is an almost 700-year-old stone bridge connecting the west with the east. The Charles Bridge is an emblem of the city's situation in Europe, the two halves of which have been seeking each other out at the very least since the bridge's foundations were laid. The West and the East. Two branches of the same culture, yet representing two differing traditions, different tribes of the peoples of Europe.

It also represents the peculiar invulnerability of this city, its capacity to recover from disasters. For centuries, it has withstood the high waters that regularly flood Prague. Only once, two centuries ago, has it suffered, when two of its arches collapsed, taking pedestrians with them into the swollen waters. But the bridge was quickly repaired, and today the citizens of Prague no longer know anything about an event that contemporary chroniclers considered one of the worst catastrophes ever to afflict the city.

*

The language spoken in Prague is unostentatious as well. It is full of the vernacular and unlike Russian, for instance, sets no great store by grand emotions. A Czech writer today would hesitate to write that his city was 'magical' or 'mystical'; he might hesitate even to think so.

In his play *Audience*, Václav Havel tried to give a name to the situation of a banned writer who has to work in a brewery, by using the refrain: 'Them's the paradoxes, eh?' The word 'paradox' also applies to the spirit of this city. Prague is full of paradoxes. It is brimming with churches, yet only a small number of practising Christians can be found there; it is proud of having one of the oldest universities in central Europe, and a population that has been literate for centuries, but there are few places in the world where learning is so underrated.

Another paradox is the structure that dominates the city: Prague Castle. It is one of the largest fortresses in central Europe (its basic ground plan was established before the era of grand defeats), a great castle that went through its last great reconstruction at a time when the ruler scarcely lived in it. Now it is the seat of presidents. Their fate reflects that of the city from which they ruled. Of the nine previous presidents, four spent more than three years in prison; a fifth was in prison for a shorter time; another (perhaps better forgotten, since most of his presidency coincided with the period of Nazi occupation) died in prison; and the three remaining escaped prison or execution only by fleeing the country. What a strange and paradoxical connection between prisons and the royal castle!

It is perhaps only in a city so full of paradoxes that, within the space of several weeks, two vastly different but brilliant writers could have been born. One was a Jew who would write in German, a vegetarian, teetotal and self-absorbed ascetic, a man so obsessed with the knowledge of his own responsibility, his mission as a writer and his own shortcomings, that he dared not have most of his works published while he was alive. The other was a drunk, an anarchist, a *bon vivant*, an extrovert who ridiculed his profession and his responsibilities, who wrote in pubs and sold his work on the spot for a few beers. Franz Kafka and Jaroslav Hašek, author of *The Good Soldier Švejk*, lived their brief lives (both died prematurely, within a year of each other) separated by only a few streets. They each drew on the same period to create works of genius, but those works seem separated not just by ages, but by continents as well. Since then the people of Prague have used the word *Kafkárna* to describe the absurdities of their lives, and have called their own ability to make light of such absurdities, to confront violence with humour and utterly passive resistance, *Švejkovina*.

*

The Prague of past eras is gone. No one can bring the murdered back to life, and most of those who were driven out will probably never return to the city. Nevertheless Prague has survived and has, finally, tasted freedom again. Its spirit is intact as well. This manifested itself vividly during the revolution that opened the way to freedom in 1989. Revolutions are usually marked by high-sounding slogans and flags; blood flows, or at least glass is shattered and stones fly. The November revolution, which earned the epithet 'velvet', differed from other revolutions not only in its peacefulness, but also in the main weapon used in the struggle. It was ridicule. Almost every available space in Prague—the walls of buildings, the subway stations, the windows of buses and streetcars, shop windows, lampposts, even statues and monuments—were covered, in the space of a few days, with an unbelievable number of signs and posters. Although the slogans had a single object—to overthrow the dictatorship—their tone was light, ironic. The citizens of Prague delivered the *coup de grâce* to their despised rulers not with a sword, but with a joke. Yet at the heart of this original, unemotional style of struggle there dwelt a stunning passion. It was the most recent and perhaps the most remarkable paradox to date in the life of this remarkable city.

RETURN TO PRAGUE:

A Conversation between Ivan Klíma and Philip Roth

PHILIP ROTH: What has it been like, all these years, publishing in your own country in samizdat editions? The surreptitious publication of serious literary works in small quantities must find an audience that is, generally speaking, more enlightened and intellectually more sophisticated than the wider Czech readership. Samizdat publication presumably fosters an unspoken and unique solidarity between writers and reader, and that could be exhilarating. Yet because samizdat is a limited and artificial response to the evil of censorship, it remains unfulfilling for everyone. Tell me about the literary culture that was spawned here by samizdat publication.

IVAN KLÍMA: Your observation that samizdat literature fosters a special type of reader seems right. The Czech samizdat originated in a situation that is in its way unique. The powers that be, supported by foreign armies—installed by the occupier and aware that they could exist only by the will of the occupier—were afraid of criticism. They also realized that any kind of intellectual and spiritual life at all is directed, in the end, towards freedom. That's why they did not hesitate to forbid practically all Czech culture, to make it impossible for writers to write, painters to exhibit, scientists—especially in the social sciences—to carry out independent research; they destroyed the universities, appointing as professors for the most part docile clerks. The nation, caught off guard by this catastrophe, accepted it passively, at least for a time, looking on helplessly at the disappearance, one after another, of people whom it had so recently respected and to whom it had looked with hope.

Samizdat originated slowly. At the beginning of the seventies, my friends and fellow writers who were forbidden to publish used to meet at my house once a month. They included the leading creators of Czech literature: Václav Havel, Jiří Gruša, Ludvík Vaculík, Pavel Kohout, Alexander Kliment, Jan Trefulka, Milan Uhde and several dozen others. At these meetings we read our new work aloud to one another. Some, like Bohumil Hrabal and Jaroslav Seifert, did not come personally, but sent their work for us to read. The police got interested in these meetings; on their instruction, the television network produced a short film that hinted darkly that dangerous conspiratorial conclaves were taking place in my flat. I was told to cancel the meetings, but we all agreed that we would type out our manuscripts and sell them for the price of the copy. The 'business' was taken on by one of the best Czech writers, Ludvík Vaculík. That's how we began: one typist and one ordinary typewriter.

The works were printed in editions of ten to twenty copies; the cost of one copy was about three times the price of a normal book. Soon what we were doing got about. People began to look out for these books, new 'workshops' sprang up, which often copied unauthorized copies. At the same time the standard layout improved. Somewhat deviously, we managed to have the books bound at the state bookbinders; they were often accompanied by drawings by leading artists, also banned. Many of these books will be, or already are, the pride of bibliophile collections. As time went on, the number of copies increased— as did the titles and readers. Almost everyone 'lucky' enough to own a samizdat was surrounded by a circle interested in borrowing it. The writers were soon followed by others: philosophers, historians, sociologists, nonconformist Catholics, as well as supporters of jazz, pop and folk music, and young writers who refused to publish officially, even though they were allowed to. Dozens of books in translation began to come out in this way, political books, religious books, often lyrical poetry or meditative prose. Whole editions came into being and remarkable feats of editing—for instance the collected writings, with commentary, of our greatest contemporary philosopher, Jan Patočka.

At first the police tried to prevent samizdats, confiscating individual copies during house searches. A couple of times they arrested the typists who copied them, and some were even sentenced to imprisonment by the 'free' courts, but the samizdat started to resemble, from the point of view of the authorities, the many-headed dragon in the fairy tale, or a plague—samizdat was unconquerable.

There are no precise statistics yet, but I know there were roughly two hundred samizdat periodicals alone and several thousand books. Of course when we speak of thousands of book titles we can't always expect high quality—but one thing completely separated samizdat from the rest of Czech culture: it was independent both of the market and of the censor. This independent Czech culture strongly attracted the younger generation, in part because it had the aura of the forbidden. We've estimated that some books had tens of thousands of readers, and we mustn't forget that a lot of these books were published by Czech publishing houses in exile and then returned to Czechoslovakia by the most devious routes.

Nor should we pass over the great part played in propagating what was called 'uncensored literature' by the foreign broadcasting stations Radio Free Europe and the Voice of America. Radio Free Europe broadcast the most important of the samizdat books in serial form, and had hundreds of thousands of listeners. (One of the last books that I heard read on this station was Havel's remarkable *Long Distance Interrogation* [published in English as *Disturbing the Peace*]—an account not only of his life but also of his political ideas.) I'm convinced that this 'underground culture' had an important influence on the revolutionary events of the autumn of 1989.

PHILIP ROTH: It always seemed to me that there was a certain amount of loose, romantic talk in the West about 'the muse of censorship' behind the iron curtain. I would venture that there were even writers in the West who sometimes envied the terrible pressure under which you people wrote and the clarity of the mission this burden fostered: in your society you were virtually the only monitors of truth. In a censorship culture, where everybody lives a double life—of lies and truth—literature becomes a life-preserver, the remnant of truth people cling to. I think it's also true that in a culture like mine, where nothing is censored but where the mass media inundate us with the most inane falsifications of human affairs, serious literature is no less of a life-preserver, even if the society is all but oblivious to it.

When I returned to the United States from Prague after my first visit to the city in the early seventies, I compared the Czech writers' situation with ours in America by saying, 'There nothing goes and everything matters—here everything goes and nothing matters.' But at what cost did everything you wrote matter so much? How would you estimate the toll that repression, which put such a high premium on literature, has taken on the writers you know?

IVAN KLÍMA: Your comparison of the situation of Czech writers with writers in a free country is one that I have often repeated. I'm not able to judge the paradox of the second half, but the first catches the paradox of our situation wonderfully. Writers had to pay a high price for these words that take on importance because of the bans and persecution—the ban on publishing was connected not only with a suppression of all social activity, but also in most cases with a ban on doing any work writers were qualified for. Almost all my banned colleagues had to earn their living as labourers. Window-cleaners, as we know them from Kundera's novel, were not typically doctors, but there were many writers, critics and translators who earned their living in this way. Others worked as crane operators, or digging on geological research sites. Now it might seem that such work could provide an interesting experience for a writer. And that's true, so long as the work lasts for a limited time and there is some prospect of escape from blunting and exhausting drudgery. Fifteen or even twenty years of work like that, exclusion like that, affects one's whole personality. The cruelty and injustice completely broke some of those subjected to it, others were so exhausted that they were simply unable to undertake any creative work. If they did somehow manage to persevere, it was by sacrificing to this work everything: any claim to rest and often to any chance of a personal life.

PHILIP ROTH: Milan Kundera, I discover, is something of an obsession here among the writers and journalists I talk to. There appears to be a controversy over what might be called his 'internationalism'. Some people have suggested to me that in his two books written in exile, *The Book of Laughter and Forgetting* and *The Unbearable Lightness of Being*, he is writing 'for' the French, 'for' the Americans, and that this constitutes some sort of cultural misdemeanour or even betrayal. To me, he seems rather to be a writer who, once he found himself living abroad, decided, quite realistically, that it was best not to pretend that he was a writer living at home, and who had then to devise himself a literary strategy, one congruent not with his old but with his new complexities. Leaving aside the matter of quality, the marked difference of approach between the books written in Czechoslovakia, like *The Joke* and *Laughable Loves*, and those written in France does not represent to me a lapse of integrity, let alone a falsification of his experience, but a strong, innovative response to an inescapable challenge. Would you explain what problems Kundera presents to those Czech intellectuals who are so obsessed with his writing in exile?

IVAN KLÍMA: Their relation to Kundera is indeed complicated and I would stress beforehand that only a minority of Czechs have any opinion about Kundera's writing for one simple reason: his books have not been published in Czechoslovakia for more than twenty years. The reproach that he is writing for foreigners rather than for Czechs is only one of the many reproaches addressed to Kundera and only a part of the more substantial rebuke—that he has lost his ties to his native country. We can really leave aside the matter of quality because the allergy to him is not produced by the quality of his writing, but by something else.

The defenders of Kundera—and there are many here—explain the animosity toward him among Czech intellectuals by an attitude towards our famous Czech compatriots that is not so rare: envy. But I don't see this problem so simply. I can mention many famous compatriots, even among the writers (Havel at home, Škvorecký abroad) who are very popular and even beloved by intellectuals here.

I have used the word allergy. Various irritants produce the allergy and it's rather difficult to find the crucial ones. In my opinion it is caused, in part, by what people take to be the simplified and spectacular way in which Kundera presents his Czech experience. What's more, the experience he presents is, one might say, at odds with the fact that he himself had been an indulged and rewarded child of the communist regime until 1968.

The totalitarian system is terribly hard on people, as Kundera recognizes, but the hardness of life has a much more complicated shape than we find in his presentation of it. Kundera's picture, his critics would tell you, is the sort of picture which you would see from a very capable foreign newspaperman who'd spent a few days in our country. Such a picture is acceptable to the Western reader because it confirms his expectations; it reinforces the fairy tale about good and evil, which a good boy likes to hear again and again. But for these Czech readers our reality is no fairy tale. They expect a much more comprehensive and complex picture, a deeper insight into our lives from a writer of Kundera's stature. Kundera certainly has other aspirations for his writing than merely providing a picture of Czech reality, but those attributes of his work may not be so relevant for a Czech audience.

Another reason for the allergy probably has to do with the prudery of some Czech readers. Although in their personal lives they may not behave puritanically, they are rather more strict about an author's morality.

Last, but not least, is an extra literary reason, which may, however, be at the very core of the charge against him. At the time when Kundera was achieving his greatest world popularity, Czech culture was in a bitter struggle with the totalitarian system. Intellectuals at home as well as those in exile shared in this struggle. They underwent all sorts of hardships: they sacrificed their personal freedom, their professional position, their time, their comfortable lives. For example, Josef Škvorecký and his wife, Zdena Salivarová, virtually abandoned their personal lives to work abroad on behalf of suppressed Czech literature. Kundera seemed to many people to have stood apart from this kind of effort. Surely it was his right—why should every writer have to become a fighter?—and it certainly can be argued that he has done more than enough for the Czech cause by his writing itself. Anyway, I have tried to explain candidly why Kundera has been accepted in his own country with considerably more hesitation than in the rest of the world.

In his defence, let me say that there is a kind of xenophobia here with respect to the suffering of the past half century. The Czechs are by now rather possessive of their suffering, and though this is perhaps understandable and a natural enough reaction, it has resulted, in my opinion, in an unjust denigration of Kundera, who is, without a doubt, one of the great Czech writers of this century.

PHILIP ROTH: The official, or officialized, writers are a bit of a mystery to me. Were they all bad writers? Were there any interesting opportunistic writers? I say opportunistic writers rather than believing writers because though there may well have been believers among the writers in the first decade or so after the war, I assume that during the last decade the official writers were opportunists and nothing more. Correct me, of course, if I'm wrong about that. And then tell me—was it possible to remain a good writer and accept the official rulers and their rules? Or was the work automatically weakened and compromised by this acceptance?

IVAN KLÍMA: It's true that there is a basic difference between authors who supported the regime in the fifties and those who supported it after the occupation in 1968. Before the war what was called leftist literature played a relatively important role. The fact that the Soviet army liberated the greater part of the Republic—and the memory of Munich and the Western powers' desertion of Czechoslovakia, despite all their treaties and promises—further strengthened this leftist tendency. The younger generation especially succumbed to illusions of a new, more just society that the Communists were going to build. It was precisely this generation that saw through the regime and contributed enormously to the Prague Spring movement and to demystifying the Stalinist dictatorship.

After 1968 there was no longer any reason for anyone, except perhaps for a few frenzied fanatics, to share those postwar illusions. The Soviet army had changed in the eyes of the nation from a liberating army to an army of occupation, and the regime that supported this occupation had changed into a band of collaborators. If a writer didn't notice these changes, his blindness deprived him of the right to count himself among creative spirits; if he noticed them but pretended he knew nothing about them, he may rightfully be called an opportunist—it is probably the kindest description.

Of course the problem lay in the fact that the regime lasted not just a few months or years, but two decades. This meant that, exceptions apart—and the regime persecuted those exceptions harshly—virtually a generation of protesters, from the end of the seventies on, was forced to emigrate. Everyone else had to accept it in some way or even support it. Television and radio had to function somehow, the publishing houses had to cover paper with print. Even quite decent people thought: if I don't hold this job, someone worse will. If I do not write—and I shall try to smuggle at least a bit of truth through to the reader—the only people left will be those who are willing to serve the regime devotedly and uncritically.

I want to avoid saying that everyone who published anything over the past twenty years is necessarily a bad writer. It's true too that the regime gradually tried to make some important Czech writers their own and so began to publish some of their works. In this way it published at least a few works by Bohumil Hrabal and the poet Miroslav Holub (both of them made public self-criticisms) and also poems by the Nobel Prize winner Jaroslav Seifert, who had signed Charter 77. But it can be stated categorically that the effort of publication, getting past all the traps laid by the censor, was a severe burden on the works of many of those who were published. I have carefully compared the works of Hrabal—who, to my mind, is one of the greatest living European prose writers—that came out in samizdat form and were published abroad, with those that were published officially in Czechoslovakia. The changes he was evidently forced by the censor to make are, from the point of view of the work, monstrous in the true sense of the word. But much worse than this was the fact that many writers reckoned with censorship beforehand, and deformed their own work, and so, of course, deformed themselves.

Only in the eighties did 'angry young men' begin to appear, especially among young authors, theatre people and writers of protest songs. They said exactly what they meant and risked their works not coming out, or even having their livelihoods threatened. They contributed to our having a free literature today—and not only literature.

PHILIP ROTH: Since the Soviet occupation of Czechoslovakia a sizeable sampling of contemporary Czech writers has been published in America: among those living in exile are Kundera, Pavel Kohout, Škvorecký, Jiří Gruša and Arnošt Lustig; and of those in Czechoslovakia, you, Vaculík, Hrabal, Holub and Havel. This is an astonishing representation from a small European country—I can't think of ten Norwegian or ten Dutch writers who have been published in the United States since 1968. To be sure, the place that produced Kafka has special significance, but I don't think either of us believes that this accounts for the attention that your nation's literature has been able to command in the West. You have had the ear of many foreign writers. They have been incredibly deferential to your literature. You have been given a special hearing and your lives and works have absorbed a lot of their thinking. Has it occurred to you that this has now all changed, and that, in the future, you're perhaps going to be talking not quite so much to us but to each other again?

IVAN KLÍMA: Certainly the harsh fate of the nation suggested many compelling themes. A writer was himself often forced by circumstances to have experiences that would otherwise have remained foreign to him and that, when he wrote about them, may have appeared to readers as almost exotic. It's also true that writing was the last place where one could still set up shop as an individual. Many creative people actually became writers for this reason alone. All this will pass to some extent, even though

I think there is an aversion to the cult of the élite in Czech society, and that Czech writers will always be concerned with the everyday problems of ordinary people. This applies to the great writers of the past as well as to contemporary ones: Kafka never ceased to be an office worker, Čapek was a journalist, and Hašek and Hrabal spent a lot of their time in smoky pubs. Holub never left his job as a scientist and Vaculík stubbornly avoided everything that might drag him away from leading the life of the most ordinary of citizens. Of course, as social life changes, so will themes. But I'm not sure this means our literature will necessarily become less interesting to outsiders. I believe our literature has pushed open the gate to Europe and even to the world just a crack, not only because of its subjects, but because of its quality.

PHILIP ROTH: And inside Czechoslovakia? Right now I know people are wildly hungry for books, but after the revolutionary fervour subsides, with the sense of unity in struggle dissipating, might you not come to mean far less to readers here than you did when you were fighting to keep alive for them a language other than the language of the official newspapers, the official speeches and the official government-sanctioned books?

IVAN KLÍMA: I agree that our literature will lose some of its extra literary appeal. But many think that these secondary appeals were distracting both writers and readers with questions that should have been answered by journalists, by sociologists, by political analysts. Let's go back to what I call the intriguing plots offered by the totalitarian system. Stupidity triumphant, the arrogance of power, violence against the innocent, police brutality, the ruthlessness that permeates life and produces labour camps and prisons, the humiliation of man, life based on lies and pretences: these stories will lose their topicality, I hope, even though writers will probably return to consider them again after a while. But the new situation must bring new subjects—in the first place forty years of the totalitarian system have left behind a material and spiritual emptiness, and filling this emptiness will be full of difficulties, tension, disappointment and tragedy.

It is also true that in Czechoslovakia a feeling for books has a deep tradition, reaching back to the Middle Ages, and even with television sets everywhere, it's hard to find a family that does not own a library of good books. Even though I don't like prophesying, I believe that, for the time being at least, the fall of the totalitarian system will not turn literature into an occasional subject with which to ward off boredom at parties.

PHILIP ROTH: The late Polish writer Tadeusz Borowski said that the only way to write about the Holocaust was as the guilty, as the complicit and implicated: that is what he did in his first-person fictional memoir, *This Way for the Gas, Ladies and Gentlemen*. There Borowski may even have pretended to a dramatically more chilling degree of moral numbness than he felt as a prisoner in Auschwitz, precisely to reveal the horror of the camp as the wholly innocent victims could not. I think that under the domination of Soviet Communism, some of the most original Eastern European writers I have read in English have positioned themselves similarly—Tadeusz, Konwicki, Danilo Kiš and Kundera, say, to name only three 'K.s who have crawled out from under Kafka's cockroach to tell us that there are no uncontaminated angels, that the evil is inside as well as outside. Still, this sort of self-flagellation, despite its ironies and nuances, cannot be free from the element of blame, from the moral habit of situating the source of the evil in the system even when examining how the system contaminates you and me. You are used to being on the side of truth, with all the risks entailed in becoming righteous, pious, didactic, dutifully counter-propagandistic. You are not used to living without that well-defined, recognizable, objective sort of evil. I wonder what will happen to your writing—and to the moral habits embedded in it—with the removal of the system: without *them*, with just you and me.

IVAN KLÍMA: That question makes me think back over everything I have said until now. I have found that I often describe a conflict in which I am defending myself against an aggressive world, embodied by the system. But I have written about the conflict between myself and the system without necessarily supposing that the world is worse than I am. I should say that the dichotomy—I on the one side and the world on the other—is the way in which not only writers, but all of us, are tempted to perceive things.

Whether it is the world or the system or individuals or luck or laws that are bad, is not really the point. We could both name dozens of works created in free societies in which the hero is flung here and there by a hostile, misunderstanding society, and so assure each other that it is not only in our part of the world that writers succumb to the temptation to see the conflict between themselves—or their heroes—and the world around them as the dualism of good and evil.

I would imagine that those in the habit of seeing the world dualistically will certainly be able to find some other form of external evil. On the other hand, the changed situation could help others to step out of the cycle of merely reacting to the cruelty or stupidity of the system, and lead them to reflect anew on man in the world. And what will happen to my writing now? Over the past three months I have been swamped with so many other responsibilities that the idea that someday I'll write a story in peace and quiet seems fantastic. But to answer the question—as far as my writing is concerned, I'm relieved that I no longer have to worry about that unhappy social system.

PHILIP ROTH: Last November, while the demonstrations that resulted in the new Czechoslovakia were being addressed by the outcast ex-convict Havel here in Prague, I was teaching a course on Kafka at a college in New York City. The students, of course, read *The Castle*, about K.'s tedious, fruitless struggle to gain recognition as a land surveyor from that mighty and inaccessible sleepyhead who controls the castle bureaucracy, Mr Klamm. When a photograph appeared in the *New York Times* showing Havel reaching across a conference table to shake the hand of the old regime's prime minister, I showed it to my class. 'Well,' I said, 'K. finally meets Klamm.' You should know that the students were pleased when Havel decided to run for president—that would put K. in the castle, and as successor, no less, to Klamm's boss.

Kafka's prescient irony may not be the most remarkable

attribute of his work but it's always stunning to think about it. He is anything but a fantasist creating a dream or a nightmare world as opposed to a realistic one. His fiction keeps insisting that what seems to be an unimaginable hallucination and hopeless paradox is precisely what constitutes one's reality. In works such as *Metamorphosis*, *The Trial* and *The Castle*, he chronicles the education of someone who comes to accept—rather too late, in the case of the accused Josef K.—that what looks to be outlandish and ludicrous and unbelievable, beneath your dignity and concern, is nothing less than what is happening to you; that thing beneath your dignity turns out to be your destiny.

'It was no dream,' Kafka writes only moments after Gregor Samsa awakens to discover that he is no longer a good son supporting his family but a repellent insect. The dream, according to Kafka, is of a world of probability, of proportion, of stability and order, of cause and effect—a dependable world of dignity and justice is what is absurdly fantastic to him. How amused Kafka would have been by the indignation of those dreamers who tell us daily, 'I didn't come here to be insulted!' In Kafka's world—and not just in Kafka's world—life only begins to make sense when we realize that it is exactly why we are here.

I'd like to know what role Kafka may have played in your imagination during your years of being here to be insulted. Kafka was, of course, banned by the communist authorities from the bookstores, libraries and universities in his own city and throughout Czechoslovakia. Why? What frightened them? What enraged them? What did he mean to the rest of you who know his work intimately and may even feel a strong affinity with his origins?

IVAN KLÍMA: Like you, I have studied Kafka's works, but I would express the conflict between the dream world and the real one in his work slightly differently. You say: 'The dream, according to Kafka, is of a world of probability, of proportion, of stability and order, of cause and effect—a dependable world of dignity and justice is what is fantastic to him.' I would replace the word 'fantastic' with the word 'unattainable'. What you call the dream world was, for Kafka, the real world—the world in which order reigned, in which people were able to grow fond of each other, make love, raise families, be orderly in all their duties—but for him, with his obsessive truthfulness, this world was unattainable. His heroes suffered not because they could not realize their dreams, but because they were not strong enough properly to enter the real world, to fulfil their duty.

The reason Kafka was banned under communist regimes is explained in a single sentence by the hero of my novel *Love and Garbage*: 'What matters most about Kafka's personality is his honesty.' A regime that is built on deception, that asks people to pretend, that demands external agreement without caring about the inner conviction of those to whom it turns for consent, a regime afraid of anyone who asks about the sense of his actions, cannot allow anyone whose veracity attained such fascinating or even terrifying completeness to speak to the people.

If you ask what Kafka meant to me, we get back to the question we somehow keep circling. On the whole Kafka was an unpolitical writer. I like to quote the entry in his diary for 2 August 1914. 'Germany has declared war on Russia.— Swimming in the afternoon.' Here the historic, world-shaking plane and the personal one are exactly level. I am sure that Kafka wrote only from his innermost need to confess his personal crises and so solve what seemed to him unsolvable in his personal life: in the first place, his relationship with his father, and second, his inability to pass beyond a certain limit in his relationships with women. For instance, his murderous machine in the short story 'In the Penal Colony' is a wonderful, passionate, and desperate image of the state of being married or engaged. Several years after writing this story he confided to Milena Jesenská his feelings on thinking about their living together:

> You know, when I try to write something [about our
> engagement] the swords whose points surround me in
> a circle begin slowly to approach the body, it's the
> most complete torture; when they begin to graze me
> it's already so terrible that, at the first scream, I betray
> you, myself, everything.

61

Kafka's metaphors were so powerful that they far exceeded his original intentions. I know that *The Trial* as well as 'In the Penal Colony' have been explained as ingenious prophecies of the terrible fate that befell the Jewish nation during the war, which broke out fifteen years after Kafka's death. But it was no prophecy of genius; these works merely prove that a creator who knows how to reflect his most personal experiences deeply and truthfully also touches the suprapersonal or social spheres. Again I am answering the question about political content in literature. Literature doesn't have to scratch around for political realities, or even worry about systems that come and go; it can transcend them and still answer questions that the system evokes in people. This is the most important lesson that I extracted for myself from Kafka.

PHILIP ROTH: You were born a Jew and, because you were a Jew, you spent part of your childhood in a concentration camp. Do you feel that this background distinguishes your work—or that, under the Communists, it altered your predicament as a writer—in ways worth talking about? In the decade before the war, Central Europe without Jews as a persuasive cultural presence—without Jewish readers or Jewish writers, without Jewish journalists, playwrights, publishers, critics—was unthinkable. Now that the literary life in this part of Europe is about to be conducted once again in an intellectual atmosphere that harks back to prewar days, I wonder if—perhaps even for the first time—the absence of Jews will register with any impact on the society. Is there a remnant left in Czech literature of the prewar Jewish culture, or have the mentality and sensibility of Jews, which were once so strong in Prague, left Czech literature for good?

IVAN KLÍMA: Anyone who has spent time in a concentration camp as a child—who has been completely dependent on an external power which can at any moment come in and beat or kill him and everyone around him—probably moves through life at least a bit differently from people who have been spared such an education. That life can be snapped like a piece of string—that was my daily lesson as a child. And the effect of this on my writing? An obsession with the problem of justice, with the feelings of people who have been condemned and cast out, the lonely and the helpless. The themes issuing from this, thanks to the fate of my country, have lost nothing of their topicality. And the effect on my life? Among friends, I have always been known as an optimist. Anyone who survives being repeatedly condemned to death may either suffer from paranoia all his life, or from a confidence not justified by reason believe that everything can be survived and everything will turn out all right in the end.

As for the influence of Jewish culture on our present culture—if we look back, we are apt to idealize the cultural reality in rather the same way that we idealize our own childhoods. If I look back at my native Prague, say at the beginning of this century, I am amazed by the marvellous mix of cultures and customs, by so many of the city's great men: Kafka, Rilke, Hašek, Werfel, Einstein, Dvořák, Max Brod . . . But, of course, Prague's past consisted not only of a dazzling number of the greatly gifted, not only of a cultural surge; it was also a time of hatred, of furious and petty and often bloody clashes.

If we speak of the magnificent surge of Jewish culture that Prague witnessed more than almost anywhere else, we must also recognize that there has never been an extended period of time here without some sort of anti-Semitic explosion. To most people the Jews represented a foreign element, which they tried at the very least to isolate. There is no doubt that Jewish culture enriched Czech culture by the very fact that, like German culture, which also had an important presence in Bohemia (and Jewish literature in Bohemia was largely written in German), it became a bridge to Western Europe for the developing Czech culture, the evolution of which had been stifled for two hundred years.

What has survived from that past? Apparently nothing. But I'm convinced that this is not the whole story. Surely the present longing to overcome the nihilist past with tolerance, the longing to return to untainted sources, is a response to the almost forgotten warning call of the dead—and indeed the murdered—to us, the living.

PHILIP ROTH: A complicated man of mischievous irony and solid intellect such as Havel, a man of letters, a student of philosophy, an idealist with strong spiritual inclinations, a playful thinker who speaks his native language with precision and directness, who reasons with logic and nuance, who laughs with gusto, who is enchanted with theatricality, who knows intimately and understands his country's history and culture—such a person would have even less chance of being elected president in the United States than Jesse Jackson or Geraldine Ferraro.

Just this morning I went to the Castle, to a press conference he held about his trips to the United States and Russia, and I listened with pleasure—and some astonishment—to a president composing, on the spot, sentences that were punchy, fluent and rich with human observation, sentences of a kind that probably hasn't been formulated so abundantly—and off the cuff—at the White House since Lincoln was shot.

When a German journalist asked whose company Havel had most preferred, the Dalai Lama's, George Bush's or Mikhail Gorbachev's—all three of whom he'd recently met—he began, 'Well, it wouldn't be wise to make a hierarchy of sympathy . . . ' When asked to describe Gorbachev, he said that one of his most attractive qualities is that 'he is a man who doesn't hesitate to confess his embarrassment when he feels it.' When he announced that he had scheduled the arrival of the West German president for 15 March, the same day as Hitler's invasion of Prague in 1939—one of the reporters noted that Havel 'liked anniversaries', whereupon Havel immediately corrected him. 'No,' he told him, 'I did not say that I "liked anniversaries". I spoke about symbols, metaphors and a sense of dramatic structure in politics.'

How did this happen here? And why did it happen here to Havel? As he would probably be the first to recognize, he was not the only stubborn, outspoken person among you, nor was he alone imprisoned for his ideas. I'd like you to tell me why he has emerged as the embodiment of this nation's new idea of itself. I wonder if he was quite such a hero to large segments of the nation when, altogether quixotically—the very epitome of the foolish, high-minded intellectual who doesn't understand real life—he was writing long, seemingly futile letters of protest to his predecessor, President Husák. Didn't a lot of people think of him then as either a nuisance or a nut? For the hundreds of thousands who never really raised an objection to the communist regime, isn't worshipping Havel a convenient means by which, virtually overnight, to jettison their own complicity with what you call the nihilist past?

IVAN KLÍMA: Before I try to explain that remarkable phenomenon called 'Havel', I'll try to give my opinion on the personality named Havel. (I hope I won't be breaking the law, still extant, that virtually forbids criticism of the president.) I agree with your characterization of him, and as someone who has met him innumerable times over the past twenty-five years, I would supplement it. Havel is known mainly as an important dramatist, then as an interesting essayist and lastly as a dissident, an opponent of the regime so firm in his principles that he was prepared to undergo anything for his convictions, including imprisonment. But in this list of Havel's skills or professions there is one fundamental thing missing.

As a dramatist Havel is placed by world critics in the stream of the theatre of the absurd. But back when it was still permissible to present Havel's plays in our theatres, the Czech public understood them primarily as political plays. I used to say, half jokingly, that Havel became a dramatist simply because, at that time, the theatre was the only platform from which political opinions could be expressed. Right from the beginning, when I got to know him, Havel was, for me, a politician first, an essayist of genius second, and a dramatist last. I am not ordering the value of his achievements but rather the priority of interests, personal inclination and enthusiasm.

In the Czech political desert, where former representatives of the democratic regime had either emigrated, been locked up, or disappeared from the political scene, Havel was really the only active representative of the line of thoroughly democratic Czech politics represented by Tomáš Masaryk. Today Masaryk lives in the national consciousness rather as an idol or as the author of the principles on which the First Republic was built. Few people know that he was an outstanding politician, a master of compromises and surprising political moves, of risky, ethically motivated acts. (One of these was the passionate defence of a poor, wandering, young Jew from a well-to-do family, Leopold Hossner, who was accused and sentenced for the ritual murder of a young dressmaker. This act of Masaryk's enraged the Czech nationalist public so much that it looked for a while as if the experienced politician had committed political suicide—he must then have seemed to his contemporaries to be 'a nuisance or a nut'.) Havel brilliantly continued in Masaryk's line of 'suicidal', ethical behaviour, though of course he carried on his political activity under much more formidable conditions than those of old Austro-Hungary. His letter to Husák in 1975 was indeed an ethically motivated but expressly political—even suicidal—act, just like the signature campaigns which he instigated over and over again and for which he was always persecuted.

Like Masaryk, Havel was a master of compromises and alliances, who never lost sight of the basic aim: to remove the totalitarian system and replace it with a renewed system of pluralist democracy. To achieve that aim he was prepared, in 1977, to join together with all the anti-totalitarian forces, whether they were reform Communists—all of them long since expelled from the Party—members of the arts underground or practising Christians. The greatest significance of Charter 77 lay precisely in this unifying act, and I have no doubt that it was Havel himself who was the author of this concept and that his was the personality that was able to link such absolutely hetero-geneous political forces.

Havel's candidacy for president and his later election were, in the first place, an expression of the precipitate, truly revolutionary course of events in this country. When I was returning from a meeting of one of the committees of Civic Forum one day towards the end of November, my friends and I were saying to each other that the time was near when we should nominate our candidate for the office of president. We agreed then that the only candidate to consider, for he enjoyed the relatively wide support of the public, was Alexander Dubček. But it became clear a few days later that the revolution had gone beyond the point where any candidate who was connected, if only by his past, with the Communist Party, was acceptable to the younger generation of Czechs. At that moment the only suitable candidate emerged—Václav Havel. Again, it was an example of Havel's political instincts—and Dubček certainly remained the only suitable candidate for Slovakia—that he linked his candidacy with the condition that Dubček should be given the second highest function in the state.

To a certain sector of the Czech public, Havel was, indeed, more or less unknown, or known as the son of a rich capitalist, even as a convict, but the revolutionary ethos that seized the nation brought about a change of attitude. In a certain atmosphere, in the midst of a crowd, however civil and restrained, an individual suddenly identifies himself with the prevailing mood and state of mind, and captures the crowd's enthusiasm. It's true that the majority of the country shared in the doings of the former system, but it's also true that the majority hated it just because it had made them complicit in its awfulness, and hardly anyone still identified himself with that regime which had so often humiliated, deceived and cheated them. Within a few days, Havel became the symbol of revolutionary change, the man who would lead society out of its crisis. Whether the motivation for supporting him was basically metaphysical, whether this support will be maintained or eventually come to be based more on reason and practical concerns, time will tell.

PHILIP ROTH: Earlier we spoke about the future. May I close with a prophecy of my own? What I say may strike you as arrogantly patronizing—the freedom-rich man warning the freedom-poor man about the dangers of becoming rich. You have fought for something for so many years now, something that you needed like air, and what I am going to say is that the air you fought for is poisoned a little, too. I assure you that I am not a sacred artist putting down the profane, nor am I a poor little rich boy whining about his luxuries. I am not complaining. I am only making a report to the academy.

There is still a pre-Second World War varnish on the societies that, since the forties, have been under Soviet domination. The countries of the satellite world have been caught in a time warp, with the result, for instance, that the McLuhanite revolution has barely touched your lives. Prague is still very much Prague and not a part of the global village. Czechoslovakia is still Czechoslovakia, and yet the Europe you are rejoining is a rapidly homogenizing Europe, a Europe whose very distinct nations are on the brink of being radically transformed. You live here in a society of prelapsarian racial innocence, knowing nothing of the great post-colonial migrations—your society, to my eyes, is astonishingly white. And then there is money and the culture of money that takes over in a market economy.

What are you going to do about money, you writers, about coming out from under the wing of a subsidized writers' union, a subsidized publishing industry, and competing in the marketplace and publishing profitable books? And what of this market economy that your new government is talking about—five, ten years from now, what are you going to make of the commercialized culture that it breeds?

As Czechoslovakia becomes a free, democratic consumer society, you writers are going to find yourselves bedevilled by a number of new adversaries from which, strangely enough, repressive, sterile totalitarianism protected you. Particularly unsettling will be the one adversary that is the pervasive, all-powerful arch-enemy of literature, literacy and language. I can guarantee that no defiant crowds will ever rally in Wenceslas Square to overthrow its tyranny, nor will any playwright-intellectual be elevated by the outraged masses to redeem the national soul from the fatuity into which this adversary reduces virtually all human discourse. I am speaking about commercial television, the trivializer of everything—not a handful of channels of boring clichéd television that nobody wants to watch because it is controlled by an oafish state censor, but a dozen or two channels of boring, clichéd television that most everybody watches all the time because it is entertaining. At long last, you and your writer colleagues have broken out of the intellectual prison of communist totalitarianism. Welcome to the World of Total Entertainment. You don't know what you have been missing. Or do you?

IVAN KLÍMA: As a man who has, after all, lived for some time in the United States, and who for twenty years has been published only in the West, I am aware of the 'danger' that a free society, and especially a market mechanism, brings to culture. Of course I know that most people prefer virtually any sort of kitsch to Cortázar or Hrabal. I know that the period when even books of poetry in our country reached editions of tens of thousands will probably pass. I suppose that a wave of literary and televisual garbage will break over our market—we can hardly prevent it. Nor am I alone in realizing that, in its newly won freedom, culture not only gains something important but also loses something. At the beginning of January, one of our best Czech film directors was interviewed on television and he warned against the commercialization of culture. When he said that censorship had protected us not only from the best works of our own and foreign culture, but also from the worst of mass culture, he annoyed many people, but I understood him. A memorandum on the position of television recently appeared which states that: television, owing to its widespread influence, is able to contribute directly to the greatest extent towards a moral revival. This of course presupposes . . . setting up a new structure, and not only in an organizational sense, but in the sense of the moral and creative responsibility of the institution as a whole and every single one of its staff, especially its leading members. The times we are living through offer our television a unique chance to try for something that does not exist elsewhere in the world . . .

The memorandum does not of course ask for the introduction of censorship, but of a supra-Party arts council, a group of independent authorities of the highest spiritual and moral standards. I signed this memorandum as the president of the Czech PEN club, although personally, I thought that the desire to structure the television of a free society in this way was rather utopian. The language of the memorandum struck me as the kind of unrealistic and moralistic language that can emerge from the euphoria of revolution.

I have mentioned that, among intellectuals especially, utopian ideas have begun to surface about how this country will link the good points of both systems—something from the state-controlled system, something from the new market system. And these ideas are probably strongest in the realm of culture. The future will show to what extent they are purely utopian. Will there be commercial television in our country, or will we continue only with subsidized, centrally directed broadcasting? And if this last does remain, will it manage to resist the demands of mass taste? We'll only know in time.

I have already told you that in Czechoslovakia literature has always enjoyed not only popularity but esteem. This is borne out by the fact that in a country with fewer than twelve million inhabitants, books by good writers, both Czech and translated, were published in editions of hundreds of thousands. What's more, the system is changing in our country at a time when ecological thinking is growing tremendously (the environment in Czechoslovakia is one of the most polluted in Europe) and it surely makes no sense for us to strive to purify the environment and at the same time to pollute our culture. So it is not really such a utopian idea to try to influence the mass media to maintain standards and even educate the nation. If some part, at least, of that idea could be realized, it would certainly be, as the authors of the memorandum say, a unique event in the history of mass communications. And after all, impulses of a spiritual character really have, from time to time, come from this little country of ours in the centre of Europe.

From the 'New York Review of Books', 12 April 1990

II

THE POVERTY OF LANGUAGE

ONE SUNDAY, WHILE I was on the bus, a man in his late middle age behind me was telling a pointless story in a loud voice. It was the kind of story you'd find hard enough to follow even if someone were telling it directly to you, and though I paid no attention to the substance of his tale, I felt an unexpected wave of disgust rise within me. It wasn't what he was saying that repelled me, it was the sound of it—his intonation, his pronunciation.

The Czech language is in decline. Every aspect of it is getting worse. The vocabulary has become impoverished and, with the exception of a few wilted metaphors that everyone has long since ceased to perceive as metaphors at all, it has lost its vividness. Spoken Czech increasingly resembles the degenerate language of journalists, for it operates within ready-made expressions and phrases.

People spew out their words—those horrible, petrified phrases—faster and more carelessly all the time, because subconsciously (and rightly) they feel that the person they are talking to will understand them anyway and that it doesn't much matter, because what they are saying isn't really saying anything.

We could, no doubt, find many causes for the decline in spoken language, all of them traceable to the evolution of civilization. The increasingly complex organization of society and structure of our knowledge demands that more and more tasks be mechanized and automated, and this means that language becomes mechanized and automated as well. Growing numbers of people, in their work, come into contact with a diminishing fragment of reality; as their world shrinks, so does their language. As our life becomes bureaucratized, so does our language. Moreover, we are surrounded by the deafening roar of impersonalized mass media, in which impoverished, clichéd speech prevails. Can the language we use in everyday intercourse possibly remain untouched by all that?

However important these reasons for the decline of language may be, they seem negligible beside another phenomenon that is more particular to this place and this time: we live and move in a milieu that is bereft of culture. I don't mean the fact that libraries have been turned over exclusively to trash, that magazines have been banned, that historians do manual labour, that national artists are not allowed to publish or show their work, that philosophers are unemployed, while muse-haters serve as artistic directors of theatres and publishing houses. I am thinking of culture in the broadest sense of the term, culture as a compendium of traditions, human rights and freedoms, culture that embraces politics and includes the right of individuals to live in unbugged privacy, to hold opinions of their own, to defend themselves if attacked. I mean culture as the habit of community spirit, the right to respect one's elders, one's wise men, and to put them in charge, the right to bury one's dead with ceremony, the right not to desecrate the graves of, or memorials to, one's ancestors. I have in mind the kind of culture that inspires an awareness of the mutability and the mystery of the world, and encourages the habit of asking questions and discussing the answers.

Here we are at the common source of culture and language, the source of the humanization of the world. Man poses questions. He questions the gods, he questions those who govern him, he questions his companions and he questions himself. And he expects answers. He may ask, for instance: is this stone instrument capable of killing a wolf?

In the long history of questioning, man has grown used to various answers. He may even consider an answer such as this meaningful: your instrument will kill that wolf if, five years ago, during the autumn equinox you bowed to the setting sun. But what if the reply tries to persuade him that his instrument is not made of stone, that it is not even an instrument; or what if they stone him to death because he bowed to the setting rather than the rising sun?

People will not be discouraged from asking questions if they get incomplete or wrong answers, but they will stop asking questions if the answers they receive are outside the order of questions asked, if those answers are misleading, confusing, mixed up and meaningless, or even threatening. But the person who stops asking questions stops thinking, for thinking is, after all, the constant asking and answering of questions. And a person who stops thinking stops talking. He emits only sounds.

In any place where culture has not yet died there remain extensive areas of mutual contact. People ask whether God or freedom or the legal order exists. They examine their own actions and the actions of their government. These questions often cause division but, at the same time, they unite people in a large human society that still needs language as a means of keeping in touch, of persisting. Wherever culture is silenced, human society perishes and language dies. In any case, this is the message of our own history, so rich in periods of suppressed culture, and in times when the national society and its languages have become moribund.

Written for a samizdat 'Festschrift', compiled for the sixtieth birthday of Bohumil Hrabal, 1974

THE END OF CIVILIZATION

EVEN WHEN I was a boy, I remember reading in magazines that within two centuries, all the coal we have on earth would be burned up, or that in 150 years we would have exhausted the last deposit of silver, or that the reserves of crude oil would hardly last us to the end of the next century. It used to seem strange to me that such details never frightened or upset anyone. People went on shovelling coal into their furnaces, and they would drive tons of steel, burning gallons of petrol, merely to convey their few kilograms from place to place.

Now, at last, the computers have worked it out for us. All this extravagance will come to an end in approximately sixty years. We will run out of food and raw materials (first zinc, tin, copper, mercury and silver, then all the rest). And so as not to arouse false hopes in some miraculous discovery that may rescue us from the coming misery, we are reminded that the water and the air will be polluted beyond recovery.

Yet moderate optimists may still be found. They don't believe what the computers predict and claim that the catastrophe will happen not in sixty years, but in ninety, or even 105. Then there are the extreme optimists and, of course, the Marxists. These people declare that nothing of the sort will happen at all. The extreme optimists claim that people have always managed to solve their problems, and the Marxists merely smile, because beneath all the shouting over the exhaustibility of our natural resources, they detect the cunning hand of bourgeois ideologists diverting the attention of working people from the intensifying class struggle. That leaves the dreamers, who propose that people should stop endlessly reproducing and pursuing higher productivity, that they should abandon the current (and clearly misguided) goals and values of industrial civilization and seek new ways of living in harmony with nature.

By now, of course, we laugh at all this. People have come to terms with their own individual death (or rather are working on ways to hasten it), so why should the death of civilization disturb their peace of mind?

Thus the end will draw near, first with apparent, then with genuine inevitability. Dreamers and prophets will increase. In some countries, where it is natural and permissible for people to associate with each other, clubs will be formed by people who have decided to walk to work or cultivate vegetables rather than roses in their gardens. Once a year, brave volunteers will block highways with their own bodies to prevent automobiles, for at least twenty-four hours, from spreading their poisonous exhaust fumes. In other countries, where association is just as natural but not permitted, there will be compulsory statewide blackouts once a week and national competitions for gathering dead branches for firewood.

Next, the first disturbing symptoms will appear. In countries where parliaments can influence the course of society, the dreamers will enforce bans on neon signs and tax products made from petroleum, tin and copper, while in countries where kings or military juntas are still in power, they will mete out punishment to irresponsible individuals who bring more than three offspring into the world. And to economize, they will make the communal viewing of television compulsory.

Meanwhile, scientists will intensify the search for new sources of raw materials and energy. They will master thermonuclear fusion and develop hundreds of new artificial substances. But it will be too late. The wonderful new inventions will remain on the drawing-board because more and more, some essential component will be lacking. Or because bringing an invention to fruition would threaten the existence of other, more essential inventions. The human spirit will languish and turn in upon itself, or towards dreaming. Our civilization will begin to resemble the body of a dying man: it may be possible to give him a new heart or liver or put fresh blood in his veins, but no one can give him back a real life.

One day the old man's life will fulfil its destiny. First the cities will die. The electrical generator in the power plant will stop, and it will cost too much to get it going again. The water mains will break and repairmen will not come to fix them. Confusion will reign in the streets, and with the night, darkness and terror will descend. The next morning, stores in which there are still goods for sale (among them now-useless items like light-bulbs, refrigerators or steering-wheel covers) will not be staffed; the assistants will have stayed at home. Some people will be so taken aback by this that they will remain in their now uninhabitable houses, awaiting death. Others will go into the streets to loot; others will try to flee. But where can they go? And how will they survive? Of what use will the knowledge and skills of a subway driver be? Or a computer programmer, a traffic policeman, a nuclear physicist or a car mechanic?

People now have a life-and-death connection with our civilization, and if it dies, they must die with it. They will die by the thousands and the millions, perhaps in famines or epidemics that can no longer be conquered, perhaps in a desperate and unwinnable war that will destroy everything.

But even if they manage to avoid war, people will die just the same. They will die of despair or because they have lost the ability to earn their daily bread or because they will have destroyed nature, which sustained them from time immemorial. Entire regions of the world will be depopulated and places that had recently radiated light will reek of the plague.

And yet, as in every disaster, human life will persist. In the end, the catastrophe will affect only one civilization. What will have imploded will be the values of only a single culture. Other cultures, after all, have managed to survive without completely succumbing to our machine civilization. They will survive with the least trauma. And with them, many of the discoveries of previous ages will persist: the invention of the wheel, the art of meditation, writing, and thus the awareness of history. Necessity will teach people to make rational and economic use of what remains of irrational and profligate civilization.

Still, the continents will drift apart once more. It will take many weeks for a sailing craft to cross the ocean and many days for a horse-drawn conveyance to cross a tract of land.

Years, centuries, millennia will pass. Highways and airports will be reclaimed by twitch grass or covered with sand. Poles supporting now-useless power grids will be toppled by winds, and birches will send shoots and branches through the windows of the still-towering skyscrapers. The air and the water will gradually become cleaner. And people's lives?

Perhaps they will become more peaceful. Mankind will return to human space and time from a world of planetary dimensions. People will enjoy silence and hear birdsong. Of course their lives will be more difficult and precarious. The foolish dream of utopians who believed that man would be made happy by being freed from the need to work will be forgotten, as will refrigerators, air-conditioning, aircraft, nuclear reactors, printing presses, artificial lungs, automatic washing-machines, television sets, rockets and bugging devices. This insane century, when man, in a meaningless effort, raised himself so high that he managed to escape the planet, will increasingly blend with legends and fables from an earlier time. One day, future scholars or priests will declare it to have been a mirage, a fiction perpetrated by ancient poets, or one of the many illusions shared by vast numbers of people. Perhaps scholarly debates on the subject will take place, but it will not affect most people because it will not touch their lives, their potentials, their goals or their happiness.

And what about their happiness? I see no reason why they should be any less happy than we who have lived in this singular and insane century.

21 April 1975

SALT—MORE VALUABLE THAN GOLD

IT BROKE OUT like a spring epidemic of the 'flu. People rushed to the shops and bought up spices and even salt, something they had already done with cocoa.

We have been through several such epidemics. Whenever there is a rumour about a currency reform, an increase in prices or the threat of war, people begin to hoard. Hoarding has a specific political and sociological meaning. Instead of the regular, controlled demonstrations of agreement and enthusiastic trust demanded by the present powers that be, the citizen here is manifesting a spontaneous and less trusting relationship. In such panic situations, he is also displaying long years of experience of the distribution system. Experience tells him he should buy what he can get, not what he happens to need at the time.

On the other hand, even a poorly informed citizen understands that a shortage of salt is unlikely. After all, they spread it on the roads in winter, and the deposits of salt in Slovakia alone will last for centuries. As for pepper, we seem to be heading for an era in which a shortage of food to put pepper on is more likely than a lack of pepper itself. The citizen, therefore, does not hoard these products because he fears a shortage of the goods in question, but because he fears a price increase. The price of spices (as with everything else) can certainly rise. But experience also tells us that as a rule, the new prices no more than double the original price. Given the present price of spices and salt, we might be talking about fractions of a crown. Moreover, as we know, salt has a tendency to become damp and then turn hard, spices lose their savour, people use them and then, after a time, throw the rest away. Even if they lay in enough to last for two or three years, they may save at most twenty or thirty crowns a year.

What fascinated me most about this whole situation was that people who often own their own homes, cars, not to mention televisions, washing-machines and other symbols of contemporary affluence, do not have the pride to rise above the salt and pepper fever. Apparently they don't consider it undignified to rush from shop to shop buying up little packages of pepper and bags of salt. In this, they manifest the wretchedness of an existence that is dominated by the frantic search for things.

I realize that dignity is not among the qualities most highly valued and sought after today. On the contrary, rather than providing man with the simple possibility of earning a living, life forces him into many undignified acts, from the humiliating questionnaires he must fill in at work, to compulsory participation in equally absurd pseudo-elections or demonstrations. At the same time, he is cast into a world where the slogan 'Grab what you can and as much as you can!' is more and more in vogue. It is a world increasingly governed by connections, corruption and illegal privileges. At the same time, he has been shut out of all activity through which he might confirm his civic and human self-respect, and denied the stimulation of contact with a living culture, with living thought, with personalities and creative acts. I understand all this and yet when I witnessed this episode with the salt and pepper, I was surprised and saddened to see how many of those who are unable to extricate themselves from the humiliating logic of the world of consumerism do not even value their own dignity above a twenty-crown note.

A natural question arises: having surrendered their dignity, how would such people behave in a genuine crisis or a real shortage? Perhaps the people who have appropriated the responsibility for the running of this society have asked themselves the same question, and have begun to understand that such episodes point not only to problems of supply, but above all, to problems of value.

20 November 1977

79

HOPE

Years ago, I was captivated by Vercors' novel *Les Animaux dénaturés* in which the author tried to pinpoint a quality that distinguished man from the animals. The quality he came up with was the capacity to create rituals, to make amulets—the capacity of a living creature to believe in a force he could turn to out of fear for his own fate.

But what good would faith in something greater than himself be if man did not cherish the hope that this higher force also took him into account?

'And now abideth faith, hope, charity, these three,' as the apostle Paul put it, 'but the greatest of these is charity.'

Of course charity or love, faith and freedom have often been denied, and people have managed to come to terms with that, but whenever man seemed denied hope, he would cling to it with his last breath.

Even a condemned man walking to his execution probably carries with him a glimmer of hope for a last-minute reprieve or a miracle. That is precisely what gives him the strength to walk to the gallows.

Hope is always connected with the future. It is the capacity of a person to imagine himself in a situation different from the one he finds himself in. What, therefore, can be more human than hope?

Death too is connected with the future. And what can be more antithetical to hope than death? In this light, hope can be seen as a vain attempt by man to avoid an awareness of the end, as temporality resisting timelessness, as a desperate attempt to drown out the silence of the universe.

Because death appears to be the only absolute in human life, all hope is relative, an illusion that helps man make it to the gallows.

Looked at absolutely, true hope can only be offered to man by someone able to invest that final necessity with hope, by someone capable of guiding man through the valley of the shadow of death.

As far as I know, the Christian God—or, more precisely, the apostle I have mentioned, speaking in His name—is the only one to have done this. No one will ever be able to judge with certainty whether the hope he offered was based on error or on inspiration, but there can be no doubt that it was the only real hope man could be given.

Ever since the way to eternal hope was opened to man, everyone who comes to eradicate God has felt the obligation to offer people a substitute, but because such hope can only with great difficulty relate to man's soul, it is usually connected with things in the world around him.

The hope of the world is to become man's hope; a hope that was inner becomes external. Man builds the world and in the resulting pandemonium the voice of his spirit, which is groaning in agony, is drowned out.

All hopes that relate to the external world, to the world of things, carry within themselves the hopelessness of their own falseness. The moment man sees through them, he turns away. But because life without hope seems scarcely bearable, he looks for new hope.

As a first glance makes clear, we live in a world that is not only flooded with machines and their by-products, but also with false hopes. And these create the circle that draws man into its deadly hopelessness.

The more passionately we cling to them, the more we will come to resemble condemned men who await a miracle while marching towards their own destruction.

December 1982

HEROES OF OUR TIME

A THOUSAND MILLION people, so they say, watched the World Cup. There may have been more or there may have been fewer, but it doesn't matter: the figure is still impressive. An unimaginable number of people sat staring at the coloured or black-and-white shadows of twenty-five mimes. They stared, and at the same time, they exercised—but what, in fact, were they exercising?

I don't know how many people followed the Federation Cup in women's tennis, but in Bohemia it seems that everyone did. Everyone wanted to see their most famous native daughter—Martina Navrátilová. She played marvellously and won everyone over, even those who tried to pretend that she didn't exist and had never existed, just as they pretend that thousands of others don't exist. Yet she returned, put in an appearance, won and, when it was over, said that she hoped she'd be back in Prague before another eleven years passed. The dignitaries wore expressions of stone when she said this, but people were delighted. They even forgave Navrátilová something rarely forgiven here: they forgave her for being rich, richer, in fact, than anyone from here can imagine. As she says herself, she keeps seven cars in her garage, among them a Rolls-Royce and a silver Mercedes-Benz.

When the super-famous Maradona scored the goal of the year with his hand and thus moved his team closer to the coveted title, some moralists took umbrage at the manner in which it was done. But an acquaintance of mine who had played professional football during the First Republic assured

82

me that Maradona could not have acted otherwise. Had he admitted scoring the goal with his hand, as befitted a hero performing before a billion people, his team-mates would probably have killed him. Did I know how many hundreds of thousands of dollars were at stake?

My acquaintance was right. Though we don't admit it to ourselves, we are watching millionaires and multimillionaires having the time of their lives.

In ancient times, a band of indigent actors arrived at Elsinore and in all humility, performed a play for the court. 'Use every man after his desert,' the Prince of the Danes says of them to Polonius, 'and who should 'scape whipping? Use them after your own honour and dignity: the less they deserve, the more merit is in your bounty.'

Today's actors whip us poor spectators and use us after their own honour and dignity.

If I speak of millionaires having the time of their lives, I am doing no more than giving a name to the present state of things. In the past, actors amused their masters. Today, the actors (or players) are the masters. Neither Maradona nor Navrátilová, however, were born masters. In fact both came from rather modest backgrounds, and if they have managed to climb up the ladder in a few years, this is a testimony to their talent, hard work and determination, certainly, but it is also a testimony to the world of today, and the depth of our longing for entertainment, or, more precisely, our longing to be entertained.

Every age has its idols and its heroes.

The times are long past when people honoured prophets or martyrs. The times are gone when audiences were entranced by names like Goethe or Ibsen. We no longer revere poets or scientists or famous inventors. We no longer whisper the names of great demagogues on our deathbeds. It even appears that the era of great movie stars and pop singers is passing away. Even the Beatles had only a handful of fans compared with Maradona.

It is a grand development. Billions watch the marvellous rushes, passes and feints, billions watch as Maradona scores a goal with his hand so cleverly that the referee doesn't see it, and thanks to that, Maradona's team goes on to the final and becomes the best in the world. Most of those watching were probably taken aback and, for a moment, felt the pangs of doubt, a kind of recollection of childhood and the world of fairy tales in which the truth triumphs, lies are unmasked and cheats punished. But a billion people also learned that such things only happen in fairy tales, that in the world we live in the Maradonas are honoured. The more diligent students among us concluded that whatever leads to victory will be justified in the end.

Victory on the playing-field, like victory in battle, has always been what counted. Anyone who does not understand that will never be successful. And success is what we are all supposed to aspire to.

How appropriate that Maradona scored a goal with his hand, and that Navrátilová has seven cars. Both of them are heroes of our age, and every age has the heroes it deserves.

September 1986

RECIPE FOR HAPPINESS

MOST PEOPLE KNOW this anonymous letter. It makes the rounds of Bohemia, and perhaps of other countries as well, at regular intervals. The text of one recently sent to me is as follows:

Chinese fortune:
Copy this letter five times and send it, along with the original, to people you think need luck. In nine days, you will see what will happen. Add your initials to the others. *[My last letter contained an unbelievable 129 two-letter initials belonging to the anonymous sponsors of Chinese fortune; the last, clearly my own sponsor in fortune, had signed with three initials—JKM.]* The original is in Spain. It has gone around the world eighty-eight times. Within nine days of receiving this letter, you will have good fortune nine-fold. But only if you send this letter on to people you think need good luck. Do not send money.
The following examples actually happened:
1) Montary Rebego received this letter, sent it on, and within nine days he won two thousand dollars.
2) Swen Romita received this letter, threw it away, and drowned within nine days.
3) J. Wiktor received this letter, forgot about it, and within nine days died in an accident.
4) In Britain in 1985, this letter was received by someone who threw it away and laughed at it. Within nine days his wife died and his son became gravely ill. He looked for the letter and sent it on. Within nine

85

days his son regained his health.

Just wait, in a few days you will have a surprise, even though you may not believe in this now.

I don't know what moves people to pass the letter on, but I would say that while some of them are guided by the altruistic motives that the foolish author of the original letter has attributed to it, most of them do so because they fear its threats. I cannot guess how many people are backward enough to believe they could bring someone fortune in this way, be it only Chinese fortune. (And why should Chinese fortune be expressed in dollars?) They probably say that it can't do any harm, after all, it's just a game—and besides, you never know. What if it's right? There are still plenty of superstitious people around. But those who take part in this chain letter may not realize that this game is less innocent than it first seems.

The text of the letter is not only facile, it is threatening. Someone who didn't have the decency to sign his name was threatening me, my wife and our children with death if I did not follow his instructions. It bristles with arrogance. Should I believe this anonymous author when he says that someone called Montary Rebego won a certain amount of money? Where and when did it happen? If he is asking for my signature, why doesn't he tell me something more precise, such as in which city, on which street and in which house this Montary Rebego lives, so that I could check that this anonymous author is telling me the truth? And what about the person from Britain? Did he really laugh at the letter, and was his wife then punished for it in a way they no longer punish even serial killers in Britain? Am I really to believe this? If I do, then I can believe anything. But I'm not being asked merely to believe this shameless drivel, I'm being asked to pass it on, for the sake of my loved ones.

The letter sounds a warning: we are losing touch with basic human decency, with the ordinary principles of ethical behaviour. At best, it suggests that people can't appreciate the meaning of a text they are apparently prepared to endorse, which means they can't even appreciate the meaning and responsibility of their own actions.

The letter now lying on my desk is evidence that 129 people, who no doubt consider themselves decent human beings, have voluntarily entered the ranks of anonymous letter-writers and spread a threatening message. But in doing so, they have done something even worse and more dangerous: they have consented to the ugly belief that you need only gird yourself with good intentions, and you can sign (though only with your initials) and send off anything that anyone presents to be believed, without having taken the trouble to verify a single claim.

I have received three such letters this year and have thrown all except one, which I only kept for the purpose of writing about it, into the waste-paper basket. When I threw out the first one, I met an interesting person with whom I spent a pleasant evening. Moreover, I felt good about not having frightened or threatened anyone. When I threw out the second one, the sun shone again after several dull, inclement days. I also received an honorarium, and a critic overseas wrote something good about me. Perhaps my declaration isn't persuasive enough, but on the other hand, I am signing it. I should add that no one close to me has died, although since the time I threw out the first letter, more than nine-times-nine days have gone by.

'Svobodné slovo', 10 October 1989

A BRIEF MEDITATION ON GARBAGE

ON MY WAY to the streetcar, I walk past a small no-man's-land. There used to be a garden here; the house it belonged to is no longer standing. A well-trodden path winds among the trees and shrubs. For years, this used to be the nicest part of my walk. Then someone threw a plastic cup on to the grass, someone else tossed away a can and someone else dumped a whole bucket of garbage. Not long ago, I realized that I was unconsciously making a detour to avoid this patch of ground, now a graveyard of junk and refuse.

Garbage interests me as a problem of our time. As a problem and as a metaphor. Once, when I was researching a novel, I worked for a short while as a street-sweeper. The city I live in has a constant struggle with garbage. The dump where most of it is taken is filling up, and no one wants to make room for another. An incinerator is being built, but it is in the middle of a populated area, and the people who live there (I would do the same in their place) are protesting that their district, which is already contaminated, will be inundated with smoke and ash from garbage produced by the rest of the city. The incinerator deals only with the consequences; the problem itself remains.

We live in an era of overproduction. The moment something is manufactured, it becomes potential garbage. It has always been that way. The difference was only in the amount and the quality of what was produced. A stone feeding-trough lasted for centuries, and a wooden brace and bit might serve several generations. A person had one pair of shoes for work and, if he wasn't an utter pauper, another pair for going to church on Sunday. A person got used to his shoes. And shoes lasted for many years. When the soles wore out, the shoemaker put on new ones. When the shoes were finally worn out, it was probably because they had succumbed to natural decomposition. But today?

We are extravagant and have given in to an almost religious worship of novelty. We get tired of things long before they wear out, and they wear out faster than they used to. Even when we don't grow tired of them, we know that they will cease to be fashionable in a matter of months after we buy them. I live in a country where, far from drowning in excess, people have been suffering from shortages, mainly a shortage of freedom. I observe now how many look with hope to a future that promises to shower them with plenty. There will be more goods and more garbage, but will there be more happiness? I doubt it. When I try to think about what can save us before we are buried in garbage, it occurs to me that someone sated with things may perhaps cease to lust after them and develop an immunity to them, the capacity to resist the dictatorship of fashion and the seductions of bright new shapes and colours, and will once more seek out quality, and in doing so, begin the journey to moderation or even modesty.

What is true of things that are apparent and visible is also true of the intellect and the spirit. The overproduction of information and ideas differs only slightly from the overproduction of things. In both cases, quantity replaces quality.

Our ancestors got along with the Bible and a few books that they not only read, but remembered. Television was unknown. The newspapers they read contained only a few pages. People were given less information, but there was more time to think things over and to observe people and nature for oneself. From this, many were able to put together a view of life that they could then embrace. But today?

We all live in a deluge of information and ideas that for the most part become garbage the moment they are created. People in Czechoslovakia not only longed for more new things, they longed for access to new information. After half a century of famine, the supply has suddenly expanded to an unbelievable degree. Left-wing and right-wing concepts are on offer, along with nationalism, anarchism, anti-Semitism and some rejigged theories about the enemy within. People buy them and discard them immoderately and, above all, indiscriminately. The things they buy seem attractive and durable, but often they are nothing more than the same old thing, revamped. I watch with alarm as people walk through the garden they once longed for without realizing that instead of walking among flowers, they walk among garbage.

I observe how they join movements, then abandon them a few months later, only to join new ones that offer more attractive but equally vacuous slogans. Crowds sometimes file past my window shouting out praises to demagogues, clinging to long-dead or utterly outmoded ideas that they have been persuaded will save them.

The flood of material garbage is something we should not take lightly. It clutters the countryside and can poison the water and the air. But intellectual garbage is more dangerous for it poisons the mind. And people with poisoned minds are capable of acts whose consequences may be irreversible.

'Frankfurter Rundschau', 29 June 1991

ON CONVERSATIONS WITH JOURNALISTS

SINCE THE VELVET Revolution, I have given many interviews to reporters from various countries and newspapers. They usually transpire in the following way: the phone rings and I hear a polite voice on the other end announcing that the person speaking has flown in yesterday, is flying out tomorrow, and would be grateful if I could find some time for her. I say yes, but ask only that the conversation stick to literature and not wander into politics or things I don't understand. I am assured that this will be the case.

In an hour (or two) the journalist appears on my doorstep. She asks if I mind if she turns on her tape recorder. I don't, and we begin. The first question has to do with problems of nationalism. I'm not an expert in such matters, but she doesn't mind, she's interested in my opinion. Very well: I answer as matter-of-factly as I know how. The second question has to do with the economic situation in the country. I'm not an expert, but she doesn't mind, she's interested in my opinion. I repeat what I heard on last night's panel discussion on television. The third question has to do with ecology. I'm not an expert, but she's interested in my opinion. Why my opinion? She doesn't reply, she merely smiles encouragingly. I offer an opinion I read last Sunday in an ecological supplement in one of the papers. I'm a little uneasy at the course the conversation is taking, but the reporter is satisfied. She still wants to know who I think will win the next election and whether the Communists are really washed up.

It took some time for me to realize that I am not asked

these questions because the questioner expects me to provide intelligent answers. On the contrary, they put such questions to me because they know I'm an amateur in the given field. In a society with highly qualified specialists in individual subjects who are amateurs in all the rest, politics—or any dilettantism, for that matter—appears to offer us a common language. And so it is routine to hear film stars talking about lifestyles, footballers thinking out loud about community affairs, and singers pontificating on questions of war and peace.

I explain to the reporter that the elections can turn out any number of ways, but I don't expect the Communists to win. She is satisfied, but suspects that I am not. She feels she ought to ask me something about my work. But what should she ask me about? She's never read a word I've written, and she's afraid she might get an opinion with more substance to it, and who would be interested in that? Then she has an idea: 'What are you going to write about now?' she asks.

Don't be misled! She is not asking me this question because she wants to learn something about my work. It is a political question, and of all the questions I am asked, it is the most frequent.

'What do you mean, "now"?'

She is somewhat taken aback. 'Well, I mean now that you have no one to fight against.'

I have tried so often to explain how writing works that I'm too tired to go over it again. So I just say, 'But I'm not a soldier.'

She doesn't understand.

'Soldiers fight. Writers write. Well or badly. Most of them badly.'

'Yes,' she says, as though she understands. 'But the conditions of your life have changed completely, so you can't go on writing about what you used to write about.'

'Why not?'

She looks at me in dismay. After all, she is the one supposed to be asking the questions. 'But totalitarianism is over.'

'What should I start writing about, then, computers? Or giraffes?'

She is confused. Until now I have answered her questions

like an obedient pupil, and now, suddenly, I've become fractious. Surely I understand what she's getting at. So far, we have struggled against totalitarianism. We wrote about persecution and the secret police, who tortured people. All that has vanished, so now we have nothing to write about, just like writers in her country.

'Do you really think they have nothing to write about?' I don't want to prolong her agony. She is merely making a common mistake about literature and life in our part of the world. She is convinced that where unfreedom reigns, the sole mission of literature is to struggle against repression, which it can only do by describing the violence and exposing its perpetrators. But because it is the outcome of a free, creative act, literature is opposed to all forms of violence, all forms of totalitarianism.

And what about life? People love and hate each other, they work, look forward to their holidays, fall ill, get well, die. They cry, laugh, enjoy themselves, are bored; they cheat each other, have deep friendships, go hungry, get drunk, tell lies and seek the confidence of others—in London, Prague, Berlin or Vladivostok. The external circumstances of their lives sometimes enter the action to varying degrees and may even form the basis of the plot, but seldom do they constitute the real essence of literature. Besides, the time in which we live—a time of transition from one system to another—provides us with more external plot material than everything in the previous era, which was bad, but almost immobile. Practically everyone used to moving through that devastated countryside along familiar pathways has now entered a landscape full of promise but largely uncharted. In some cases, euphoria has been replaced by anxiety and helplessness, even by nostalgia for the bad old days. In other cases, moderation has been replaced by greed. Corruption of unimaginable dimensions is now visibly unravelling the moral fabric of society, because of the amount of property that is changing hands and because it is up to a handful of officials to decide who can own what. People who were persecuted by the former regime are mostly poor, whereas those who persecuted them, those who were in power, are rich, and the market system favours the rich. Hope for a just settlement of past wrongs is rapidly evaporating. What can be more exciting and fascinating for a writer than a time full of such contradictions?

Yet what produces good literature is neither oppression nor freedom, nor even the most fascinating social situation. Greatness in literature depends on the talents of those who create it. Tolstoy and Chekhov lived in unfreedom, Faulkner and Greene in freedom. Marquez somewhere in between . . .

The reporter gets up and thanks me for the interview. She wants to visit some other writers as well. I don't ask her why, though I suspect I know. She wants to ask them: 'And what will you write about now?'

'Frankfurter Rundschau', 2 November 1991

ON HONESTY

FOR YEARS I was unable to leave my country and for years I watched as dishonesty grew around me. I associated it, to some extent at least, with the system that called itself socialist. In this country, everyone felt cheated and therefore justified in cheating others. I could even observe the evolution of something approximating a set of rules. As long as a thief behaved according to this code, he was not considered a thief. One stole from common property, and then of course one stole, on a small scale, from customers. But here distinctions were made between familiar and unfamiliar customers, and unfamiliar customers were subdivided into locals and foreigners. The foreign customer was robbed most of all because, if he came from the West, he was rich (and it is proper to take from the rich and give to the poor), and if he came from the East, he was considered an enemy and therefore fair game. Any foreigner who came to visit me by taxi usually paid three times the going rate for local customers. This made me feel ashamed, and I planned to write something about taxi-drivers, but meanwhile the revolution took place, the taxi-drivers raised fares for foreigners to five times the going rate, and I began to travel abroad.

In a luxury hotel in Mexico City, they added some items from the mini-bar in the room to my bill. It was a paltry amount, about twenty US dollars. When I objected on the grounds that I hadn't taken anything from the bar, I received a scornful look, but the amount was subtracted from my bill and that was that. I learned that they had charged another member of the delegation for the use of the tennis courts, although he had never held a tennis racket in his life. And they charged someone else who did not have a car for parking in the garage. If anyone protested, they would simply deduct the imaginary charge, and that was that. By way of explanation, I reminded myself that Mexico was a developing country and wasn't far from socialism.

Sometime later, in Edinburgh, a hotel added a lunch and a dinner to my bill. When I objected that I had neither lunched nor dined, they struck out the amount (it was more than in Mexico; Scotland is not a developing country) and that was that. In a shop in the same city a shopkeeper to whom I'd given a fifty-pound note tried to give me change for a twenty. When I pointed out that the change didn't seem right, she tried for a bit to persuade me (an ignorant foreigner) that it was correct, then reluctantly handed me the remaining thirty pounds, and that was that. I was beginning to understand. A gentleman doesn't check the bill. He hands over his credit card and signs the receipt. If he notices any discrepancies, he's not about to argue over a mere twenty or thirty pounds.

Several weeks ago, in Seville, I paid for a meal with a ten-thousand-peseta note and was given change for a thousand. I didn't notice until several minutes later, but by that time it was too late; the extra money was no longer in the till. The waitress had made nine thousand pesetas, and that was that. It upset me—I even wanted to write to the manager of the hotel about the dishonesty of one of his employees, but my friends dissuaded me. They said it wouldn't give a good impression, I wouldn't get the money back anyway, and they'd think I wasn't a gentleman.

I know that people have been stealing for aeons. All the ancient criminal codes provide for the punishment of thieves. And in the folklore of most nations we find licensed robbers— Robin Hoods who stole from the rich and gave to the poor. But in earlier times, there were fewer rich and more poor, and this naturally limited the number of thieves. Today, the rich are increasing and the thieves are beyond counting. Moreover, they don't give to the poor any more. They think they are the poor and so they steal with a clear conscience.

In the past, gold could buy you almost anything, but other

values counted too: dependability and honesty, a good name and decency were things people would not exchange for any material treasure. In today's frantic search for money, it seems to me that we are losing more and more of our inhibitions. All our standards of honesty and our moral principles have been shaken. The citizen today constantly sees himself in the light of dozens of the privileged, who are no longer princes in their family castles, but twenty-year-old rich kids drowning in millions because they are good at kicking a football, twanging a guitar, singing primitive songs, playing tennis or racing cars. Perhaps most of them achieved their incomes after concerted effort and a lot of hard work, but doesn't a hotel waitress (in her own eyes at least) also work hard? And what does she make in comparison with the big stars? I'm convinced that when the waitress discovered I hadn't noticed how she'd cheated me of nine thousand pesetas, she didn't feel the slightest guilt; on the contrary, she probably felt good because it meant there were fewer wrongs and more justice in the universe.

I am genuinely upset at how the borders between honesty and dishonesty are being blurred, at how dependability is vanishing from the world, at how more and more people are becoming petty thieves without a trace of conscience. One Robin Hood is bearable, even worthy of immortality in legend. But a world in which a Robin Hood stands behind every second cash-register or in every second ticket-booth, a world in which such people serve us, convey us from place to place or entertain us—such a world is scarcely bearable. Of course we have the option of behaving like gentlemen and ignoring them. The question is, will there be any gentlemen left in this world?

'Frankfurter Rundschau', 30 November 1991

III

THE POWERFUL AND THE POWERLESS

When I was still a child, I experienced a state of society in which some—the powerless—were placed at the mercy of others—the powerful. It was generally accepted that there were some who could be deprived of any rights whatever: the right to free movement, to life, even to a dignified funeral. In our part of the world, everyone has had some personal experience of this state of societal justice, or rather injustice. Just as our fathers' generation was fascinated by social problems, my generation was fascinated by the problem of justice or, more precisely, by the criminal suspension of justice by those in power. The depression of the early thirties showed our optimistic fathers the helplessness of individuals faced with poverty, unemployment and hunger. The Nuremberg laws, the Moscow trials, Auschwitz and Vorkuta opened my generation's eyes to the desperate helplessness of the individual faced with the criminal or murderous tyranny of the totalitarian state. The previous generation's groundless faith in unlimited economic development was disappointed, as was my generation's naïve belief that society would be reorganized along utopian lines. Every generation likes to think of its experience as unique and of its achievements and catastrophes as epoch-making and unprecedented, and this hampers it in assessing the real dimensions and significance of what it achieved, and what it lost.

*

None of the modern crimes against humanity—show trials, prearranged verdicts condemning innocent people to death, slave labour, mass executions, the slaughter of entire nations—

99

is an invention of this century. We can find the same thing in whatever historical era we examine. The courts that tried Socrates, Jan Hus, Jeroným of Prague, Giordano Bruno, Camille Desmoulins, Marie Antoinette or Dreyfus, as well as the thousands of tribunals that hounded heretics, dissenters or other 'traitors' and reformers, were not motivated by a desire to seek the truth. They made no effort to understand, let alone judge, the real circumstances of the indictments. They merely attempted to support and serve the existing power structure and to punish anyone it singled out for prosecution. They punished that person cruelly, as a warning, to instil terror in everyone who dared to think his own unregulated thoughts. They knew their verdicts before they knew what the essence of the dispute was (something they could not even admit, let alone deal with), before they saw the documents, or the face of the accused.

I needn't dwell on slave labour—after all, until two centuries ago (for Russians and for blacks in the western hemisphere, it was only last century) slavery was familiar to most of the world's population.

And the murder of entire groups or even nations of people? History provides enough examples of genocide. The Bible is full of stories about the slaughter of the populations of entire kingdoms and principalities, including women, children and even domestic animals. Thousands of innocent citizens were executed during the great French revolution. Entire tribes of Native Americans were wiped out in the last century—in a country that governed itself according to one of the most liberal and democratic constitutions of its time.

We should never forget that the history of the human tribe is cruel. And we should realize that what we call culture, civilization, humanism or legality is no more than a thin skin barely covering a bloody essence. It would be naïve to believe that the forces determining human behaviour for centuries have been tamed because we have, in part at least, determined what they are and named them. And yet several recent generations have succumbed again to the illusion that humanity was entering a new epoch: an epoch of material and intellectual affluence, a period when ideals that have been declared (and betrayed) for decades, if not centuries—ideals such as love, brotherhood, equality before the law and basic civic freedoms—have at last been brought to life and there is no one left who would dare betray them openly.

*

Throughout history there runs a struggle between the powerful and the powerless, between the strong and the weak. The powerful are the pharaohs of Egypt; the powerless are the small tribes of Israel. The powerful are the Romans; the powerless are the brave but isolated Carthaginians. The powerful are the feudal lords; the powerless are the numerous but badly organized serfs. The Catholic Church was powerful; the scattered truth-seekers who vainly called on the power of the Word against the sword were powerless. The Council of Constance was powerful; Jan Hus was powerless. The American colonists were powerful and the Indians, who fought with bows, arrows, a few outmoded guns, and desperate determination against cannons and an organized army, were powerless. The Gestapo was powerful, and the Jews and the citizens of subjugated countries were powerless. Every modern state is powerful, particularly a totalitarian one that not only owns all the weapons (of truly terrifying power), but also the means of economic and intellectual control; the citizen, who has only a single vote and a merely theoretical right to express an opinion about how the state should be run, is powerless.

The strength of the powerful[1] never (or almost never) derives from some higher mandate, or from spiritual values, or because they had a corner on truth or wisdom, though the powerful may have tried to claim this. It comes only from a preponderance of strength. This strength is then generally based on the number of souls dominated, on the power of their weapons and on their ability to organize.

It is true that sometimes the triumph of the powerful has foreshadowed their defeat, just as the defeat or death of the powerless has foreshadowed the triumph of their party, their position or their faith. The Roman Empire passed away, the heirs of the Christians survived and preserved something, at least, of the faith of their martyred forefathers. Jan Hus may yet be canonized. There were times in history when the former feudal nobility quaked in fear of their serfs, just as former capitalists feared their workers.

But even if their grateful descendants were to erect golden monuments to their memory, even if they were to declare them posthumously to be gods or saints or national heroes, the fact remains that these people were murdered, their unique and irreplaceable lives were wasted and cut off somewhere in their prime: Socrates, Christ, Jan Hus, Giordano Bruno, Camille Desmoulins, Isaak Babel, Osip Mandelstam, Boris Pilynak, Father Kolbe, Josef Čapek, Vladislav Vancura, Karel Poláček. And with them thousands of others, often the most decent, honest and authentic spirits of their time. They died on the crosses of occupiers, in the flames of the Inquisition, under the guillotine of the first revolution, before the firing-squads of the second revolution (counter-revolution), or in the camps of the tenth revolution. From the point of view of raw, brutal power, all these people were powerless. Their kingdom was not of the world of that power. In it, other values and other relationships held sway, and we can only ask what would have become of the world, and of all of us, had they not been prematurely silenced.

*

In most legal codes, the laws make a distinction between murder and manslaughter. In the latter case, a man may kill another man in self-defence or by mistake, in anger or when the balance of his mind is suddenly disturbed. Even after committing such a terrible act, he may return to the ways of humanity. A murderer, on the other hand, kills with deliberation, out of hatred, fanaticism or greed. He kills to achieve a premeditated goal. A murderer has deliberately left the ways of humanity and his return to a path he intentionally abandoned may well be extremely difficult.

We find the same, or a similar, distinction in even the cruellest actions taken by the powerful against the powerless. Stronger nations push out weaker ones, at the same time humiliating, enslaving and slaughtering them. Organized divisions of Romans and aggressive tribes of Germans and wild bands of Avars marched through Europe. They fought for territory, herds, crops, gold, prisoners. They plundered and pillaged, sometimes

killing everything that lived and sometimes generously leaving
the defeated alive or enslaving them. They spread terror before
them and left it in their wake. Yet there is a difference between
their actions and the actions of an Inquisition which selects its
victims according to a precise plan and tortures them, breaking
their bodies on the rack in order to break their consciences and
spirits, murdering in cold blood all those who resist. There is a
difference between the bloody acts of North American colonists
who, in moving west, battled constantly against poorly armed
and essentially helpless native tribes, and the behaviour of the
Nazi police machinery that, in a planned and cold-blooded
fashion, murdered several million European Jews.

One may rightly object: what difference does it make to the
victim whether he is murdered or merely killed? Indeed, the
difference is important only to those who survive, and it is
important for their return to humanity. A power that deliberately
decides, for its own profit, to commit murder remains a criminal
power even if it subsequently alters its morals, tries to forget its
past, or rejects that past. A criminal power was, is, and will
remain, a danger to all human society.

Fear has always been one of power's most faithful allies.
Who can imagine the terror of citizens inside a besieged city, the
terror of women when the enemy is climbing over the walls? Fear
lay down in a thousand beds the moment the inquisitors arrived
in medieval cities. And what of the anxiety in Jewish families the
day those monstrous race laws came into effect? What about the
terror of the black people when the fires of the Ku Klux Klan
burned? The breathless fear of the early dawn alive with the silent
searching of hired killers and sadistic executives of arbitrary, totalitarian power: in fascist Italy, in Nazi Germany, in Franco's Spain,
in Stalin's Soviet Union, in the Bohemian and Moravian pro-
tectorate, in Paraguay, Argentina, Uganda, Chile, Iran, China,
Yemen, Ethiopia, Indonesia, Peru, Cuba, Afghanistan and
Cambodia? How many countries are there where people have not
known the bitter taste of deadly dawns, where they have never
had to watch, with bated breath, while the fanatical messengers of
death danced beneath their very windows?

The attacker always knew that terror preceded his arrival.
He knew too that real fear saps manliness, creates panic and

cripples opposition. This is why he used it. He launched sudden ambushes, donned terrifying masks, he yelled, shrieked, waved firebrands, uttered threats, beat on the drums, banged pot lids, arranged his soldiers in formations that made their number look greater, put death's-head badges on his cap and sirens under the wings of his aircraft. There is not a power on earth that has not relied on some form of terror. Man lived not merely in fear of invaders who would ride furiously in from the distance, he lived in fear of gods or of God and his representatives on earth. He lived in fear of the authority of officers and of the bailiffs of his own masters, in fear of losing his home or the food he needed to stay alive or his land or his work.

Every effort to liberate man has in fact been an effort to liberate him from fear, to create conditions in which he would not feel his dependency as a threat. The more murderous and the more total power is, the more it deprives man of freedom and engenders fear.

If power becomes so total that it can commit any arbitrary act, can falsely accuse anyone, arrest, try and sentence him for imaginary crimes, confiscate his property, his job, his freedom and, on top of it all, publicly dishonour him with insults, then fear can also become so total that almost none of those things need actually be done to maintain it. The powers that be need only occasionally demonstrate that they are willing and able to behave arbitrarily. We live in a world in which the powerful govern by means unlike anything humanity has ever known. They can control and exterminate individuals and entire peoples. As long as these means exist, our world will remain a world of fear.

The fear that sleeps in the beds of the powerless gives a strong impetus to their dreams and their actions. The powerless person longing to escape his anxiety usually sees only two ways out: to flee beyond the reach of the hostile powers, or to become powerful himself. Fear engenders dreams of power.

There is, after all, nothing impersonal about power. It resides in people, in their behaviour and their social position. An emperor, a king, a first secretary or a prime minister all belong to the human race, try as they may to persuade us that that they are of divine origin or, at least, that they enjoy the special protection of providence. But one day they are dragged out to face the executioner, who cuts off their head; or, if they are already dead, they are dragged from the grave as proof of their human, their worldly essence. Everything essentially human is attainable; one only has to find the means of drawing power to oneself, pulling it down from heaven, stealing it from those who have it now. To the powerless, the vision of attaining power promises liberation from the shackles of fear; it promises freedom and worldly goods as well.

We have already said that power depends on strength, and strength depends on numbers, organization and effective weapons. In this way, powerless Christians who were thrown to the lions, tortured and murdered, who talked about the kingdom that was not of this earth where another order of values not recognized here held sway, grew in number and organization until one day they controlled not only monasteries and priests, but also castles and troops of armed crusaders, and in their bosom was born the symbol of the most fanatical power—the court of the Holy Inquisition.

Thus, too, the helpless proletariat, over whose cruel lot enlightened men of the last century wrung their hands, organized themselves more and more effectively until one day, at least in one part of the world, their party overthrew the government of the king, deprived him of his head, and took over the government itself, to create, or at least to declare, a life free of poverty and anxiety. Yet within a few short years first their enemies, then members of their party and finally their leaders would tremble in terror in the early morning hours, and hundreds of thousands of innocent people would be executed or die in the frozen wastelands of prison camps scattered throughout the country.

Those among the powerless who dream of saving the world through their own rule and ridding it (and themselves) of fear, are deceiving themselves. Humanity will not be redeemed by power wielded by the formerly powerless, for their innocence will be lost the day they become powerful. The moment they begin to fear the loss of their as yet unconsolidated power, their unrealized dreams and plans, they will bloody their hands and sow terror around them, and they will also reap the harvest.

They cannot escape fear. They will live in fear of revenge, of being cast back whence they came, and they will be horrified at their own acts. Power combined with fear produces frenzy. The power of the formerly powerless is often more savage than the power exercised by those they overthrew, because although those who hold it may have taken control of the government, they are still themselves haunted by fear.

*

Sometime around the middle of this century people living in the Euro-American region of the world once again embraced the foolish illusion that they (genuinely, this time) were entering the promised land. This illusion was based on the false assumption that they had essentially managed to solve the most basic social problems: how to guarantee people a decent living, offer them the chance to realize their worldly dreams without too much effort, and enjoy the gifts of life: eating, drinking, travelling and living to the full. In fact they achieved nothing of the sort: an extravagant lifestyle was attained for one or two generations of a tiny percentage of mankind, but at the cost of the unimaginable devastation of the entire planet and the squandering of energy stored up over millions of years. We can scarcely imagine the price we have paid for such an illusion. I am not thinking of ecological crimes alone, which our grandchildren's grandchildren will still be wrestling with (if they survive at all), but of something far worse.

In its efforts to organize the greatest number of forces to 'overcome nature', to 'suppress its enemies', to promote 'further growth' or to 'defend gains already made', modern society has generated huge administrative, military and police structures. These were intended to serve society, its citizens and every individual, who was to be recognized as the source of their power which was merely delegated to them. In the beginning they did no doubt recognize this. But then these structures began to behave like everyone to whom power is delegated: they began to usurp it for themselves, to the detriment of those from whom it originally derived. Certainly, there are societies where such structures are subject to some kind of control, but in most countries they are not. They are no longer governed: they govern. Unlike earlier usurpers of power, these power structures have no face, no identity. They are invulnerable to blows and to words. Their power is perhaps less ostentatious, less openly declared, but it is omnipresent and constantly growing. Those who represent it may appear in public or remain in the background, but the important thing about them is that they can be removed and replaced at any time: generals commanding an army rocket division, presidents of multi-national corporations, first secretaries of self-appointed parties or heads of the secret police.

Watching them from time to time as they wave at us from our television screens, we may suspect that compared with the power these people wield, the power of the divine pharaohs and emperors was no more than a trivial game. Nevertheless, we persuade ourselves that this is how it ought to be, that they embody the direction we are taking; they are defending our interests, serving our needs, safeguarding our security, our progress, our affluence, or whatever flashy and mendacious labels we give to our own preposterousness. What we fail to realize is that they are no longer acting in our name. We cannot get rid of them. They recognize neither a deity above them nor people below them. They recognize only themselves, their apparatus, their organizations and their own laws of motion, their destructive proliferation. They control a technology that can transform the face of the earth, that provides them the means to rule it and the arms to destroy it.

As we look on while the first two possibilities become a reality and forces gather for the third, we continue to believe that they will never do it, because they would be acting against themselves.

But every power structure that gets out of control, every murderous authority determined to abandon its humanity in order to continue growing, flourishing and swelling in a vain longing for absolute size and absolute licence, for godlike perfection, is playing with suicide.

The Roman emperors, Napoleon, Hitler and Stalin all behaved suicidally from the point of view of maintaining their power. If those who continue their work are not restrained by a human arm or the hand of fate, they can scarcely be expected to restrain themselves. But what can we, who are far more powerless, do to restrain those who have already put themselves beyond our reach, beyond the reach of our words, our pleas and our threats? We who govern nothing but our own lives, or rather— because they even have our lives in their hands—our own spirits?

*

Power is soulless and it is derived from soullessness. It builds on it and draws its strength from it. Soullessness keeps company with fear. People who have given up their souls have only a body, and it is the body they are terrified for. They are afraid of losing the creature comforts that still remain: peace and quiet, material things, convenience, luxuries. People who have not given up their souls can overcome fear because they know that in the end, fear comes from within and not from without. The person who has let anxiety from the external world replace his soul can never drive out his fear. Anyone who has defended his soul, his inner integrity, and is prepared to surrender everything, to risk even his freedom of movement and, in extreme need, even his life, cannot be broken by fear and is thus beyond the reach of power. He becomes free, he becomes a partner of power, not as a competitor in the struggle for control of the country, people and things, but as a living reminder of the mendacity and the transience of everything power defends and represents.

Those who represent soulless power cannot, of course, understand the motives of people who seem inexplicably to have broken rank. They assume the latter have the same goals as they do, and they explain their actions as the advice of an invisible demon, an Antichrist whispering in their ears, hungry for power. But there is one thing they understand right away: these isolated rebels disturb the unison of the terrified. The powerful, therefore, with all their might and using all the means they possess, will attempt to put the rebels back where they think they belong: in the emptiness where fear reigns.

When Hus stood before the Council of Constance, they did not try to persuade him, or debate with him; they simply asked him over and over again to recant. They made him his final offer when he was already tied to the stake. Did they, who refused to discuss the matter or hear any proof of truth, make this offer because they were concerned to save the life of a single little-known theologian? Not at all: they only knew that a Hus who gave up his truth and surrendered to fear, a Hus who would return to their kingdom of power humbled, would no longer represent any threat to them. A Hus who did not do this, whether alive, or burned to death, would remain a challenge to their world, to their murderous government. That is what happened, and it still goes on to this day.

A person who, out of inner need, consistently stands up to the powerful, risking everything, has a single, small hope: that by his actions, he will remind those in power where that power came from, what its origins are and what their responsibility is, and perhaps he will make them a little more human. Yet to those in power, and to those who have surrendered to it, such a goal seems like utter folly.

To the powerless, however, our hopes are concealed in the behaviour of those fools.

January 1980

¹I am treating this only from the point of view of strength. Obviously, the powerful, and those who govern, also do a great deal that is necessary and useful to the common good.

CULTURE VS. TOTALITARIANISM

WITH THE EXCEPTION of two brief periods, Czechoslovakia lived under the rule of totalitarian power for an entire half-century. The brutal tyranny of the Nazis was followed—after a three-year hiatus—by a Stalinist dictatorship. Then, after a short, more liberal period in the late sixties, the country was occupied by the Soviet Union, which renewed the totalitarian system with the help of a collaborationist government. Though the degree of cruelty and brutality varied in each decade of that half-century, what remained constant were the strictures on culture. Only cultural expressions that did not pursue freedom, a higher and better state, were allowed. In that sense it was not genuine culture at all. How did real culture, or more precisely, the cultural élite, behave under those conditions and circumstances?

On the surface, totalitarian power tried to appear as the provider of a meaningful and creative life. In fact it declared itself the liberator, leading humanity (always dissatisfied with the given state of things) towards a better future. Totalitarian power, therefore, acted as an agent of culture, claiming to provide unprecedented opportunity for cultural development. It promised scientists tranquillity for their work; it promised artists new subjects to inspire them; it promised the broad public social security and material support. Its arguments were persuasive. Instead of defending freedom as something they could not not live without, the cultural élite helped to destroy it. Many went on thinking of themselves as poets and heirs of Archimedes, and tried to get on with their work. But when totalitarian power revealed its true nature, when it manifested

110

not just its lack of culture, but its hostility to real culture, the real poets and inheritors of Archimedes began to stand out from those who had begun instead to conform because it suited their inner nature.

The invasion of my country in August 1968 was a singular act in modern history: it was the only time a foreign country had intervened militarily in the peaceful affairs of a neighbour to which it was allegedly tied with bonds of friendship. The invasion was, of course, traumatic for most citizens. Tens of thousands fled the country, many of them members of the country's intellectual élite. But the shameful nature of the invasion indelibly tarnished all those whose intention it was to renew the old-style totalitarian power. As I have said, the appearance of being cultured and civilized is particularly important in the Czech lands, where centuries of national and cultural repression have made culture, and especially literature, popular and highly respected. The powers-that-be needed poets to cloak their intentions and actions in verse. They even needed Archimedes, in whose circles they could enmesh people. But they needed them pliant, or even broken. They needed a culture that, in the words of Václav Havel, would never go beyond 'the framework of an essentially mendacious social consciousness, both transmitting and receiving as an authentic experience of the world only the appearance of such an experience.' The powers-that-be were usually able to win over a part of the intellectual élite through promises, bribery, concessions and sometimes even by force. But how could a power that was indelibly tarnished win them over? It could not. It sensed its own isolation and therefore decided to use compulsion. The early seventies were a turning-point for both the powers-that-be and for Czech culture. The regime decided to break those who, in their eyes, represented that culture, even at the cost of destroying the culture altogether. For their part, the members of the intellectual élite decided that they would rather be destroyed than have anything to do with this indelibly tarnished power.

It would be hard to find, in the history of modern totalitarian systems, such a stark polarity, such a concerted attack on a national culture and such a clear decision on the part of the élite to accept any fate rather than cooperate with the powers-that-be. In a single year, practically all the faculties of arts in the universities were destroyed, scientific and scholarly institutes were scattered to the winds, all magazines and journals dealing with the arts and culture were forbidden. Most Czech journalists, writers and academics found themselves on the Index. Their work could not be published, their existing books were removed from bookshops and libraries, and their names could not be mentioned in public, unless to disgrace them. They voluntarily became workers—as warehousemen, window-cleaners, street-sweepers, stokers and night-watchmen. Those in power thought that they would rid themselves for ever of people who might expose their true nature, who might address them and the whole of society truthfully. They had the power to banish them, but they had no power to break their spirits, and they did not dare murder them—the international atmosphere would not have allowed it. The powers-that-be believed that, in time, they would replace genuine culture with their own obedient and servile pseudo-culture. They were convinced that they would manage, as they had in the past, to get the younger generation on their side. They did not realize that they were far too unappealing to attract anyone. In their arrogance, they did not notice that not a single person of any credibility was on their side. They were not even aware that in the given state of affairs, that fateful moment of choice between themselves—now indelibly tarnished—and the values that they denied, between the repressed culture they represented and true culture, could only be repeated. Only a genuine culture could lead the nation out of the crisis, and give it back its identity and its freedom. Thus power locks itself into a charmed circle from which there is no escape, the circle of apparent, and therefore enforced, stability. But, in the words of the Czech philosopher Erazim Kohák, 'Today's enforced stability guarantees tomorrow's destabilization.'

At first, the strength of the blow against Czech culture stunned and depressed society, and it apparently sank into apathy. Nevertheless, the very people who were supposed to have been destroyed or broken realized that their situation was not hopeless. Very few of the tens of thousands who were humiliated in this way begged for mercy. Of the hundreds of forbidden writers only three purchased the privilege of publishing by indulging in public self-criticism. True culture—humiliated, repressed and banned—did not vanish from the world the way the powers-that-be had imagined, but gradually, though with great difficulty, found a way to go on existing and exercising an influence.

Gradually, the number of those trying to escape from the trap set for them by an apparently omnipresent power increased. Little groups of people began meeting in different places—on church premises, in sports clubs and, of course, in private homes. Often such groups did not know of each other's existence, but they all had a similar aim: to give life, which the powers-that-be were trying to reduce to mere biological survival, a meaning that transcended the personal.

The groups that were driven underground had to overcome many disadvantages. They were harassed, persecuted, denied access to modern communications techniques, fragmented and denied the possibility of making a living through intellectual activity. But they did have some advantages over the powers-that-be. There were several remarkable and charismatic personalities among them. These people gained in moral authority and, for everyone who longed for a meaningful life, for a life in truth, they came to personify hope in a change for the better. And, especially for the younger generation, their efforts had the appeal of something that was forbidden or even persecuted.

In 1975, two excellent texts that set the course for further action were written, and copies of them spread rapidly. One was an open letter to Dr Husák by Václav Havel, the other a collection of studies called *Heretical Essays* by the leading Czech philosopher, and later the first spokesman of Charter 77, Jan Patočka.

The first essay was a brilliant analysis of the existing system and a prediction of the collapse that its anti-human and anti-cultural stance would cause. The second essay set out the scope and aims of a struggle, the possibilities open to culture and intellectual people. Patočka figuratively characterized that struggle as 'the solidarity of the shaken'. This, he said, 'can and must create a spiritual authority and become a source of power in its own right, one that can push the warring world to accept certain limitations and then to outlaw certain acts and measures.

The solidarity of the shaken must be built amid persecution and uncertainty . . . Humanity does not reach a state of peace by surrendering and submitting to the standards of the commonplace and its promises. Anyone who discourages this solidarity must realize that he is feeding war and is a parasite . . . living on the blood of others.'

The cultural opposition understood its possibilities and its limitations. As is typical in every cultural movement, it relied chiefly on individuals. The fact that totalitarian power jealously guarded what it considered the most reliable instrument of government—that is, the right to organize—made the opposition's stress on the individual as an indispensable force in history even more important. The cultural opposition also understood that it must never enter the territory where the powers-that-be felt most at home, that is, the territory of force and violence. It understood that its one hope was to confine the struggle to where the powers-that-be could not fight back; that is, the territory of the mind and spirit. It was this that gave the resistance its non-violent character, and it predetermined the nature of the 'velvet' revolution fifteen years later.

Totalitarianism correctly understood the threat this cultural resistance posed, but the nature of that power ruled out any accommodation or compromise. It continued its battle against literature. It raided private flats and detained people who had gathered there to listen to lectures or the reading of a play or something as innocent as lyric poetry. It confiscated manuscripts from poets, prose writers and philosophers, both local and translated works, just as it did documents from Charter 77. From time to time it held trials in which judgement was passed on those who copied texts or organized other kinds of cultural activity. Because these people were clearly innocent, even according to the laws in force, the outcome of these trials was the opposite of what the authorities intended. They were meant to intimidate, but they succeeded only in unmasking power, in revealing it for the unprincipled, prejudiced and philistine force it was. This merely stiffened people's resistance. Early samizdat publications came out in tiny editions of tens of copies; by the eighties, books were being reproduced in many workshops, the technology of reproduction was modernized, and the number of titles mushroomed. (The literary samizdat enterprise Padlock Editions published three hundred titles). In the seventies, there were practically no samizdat cultural journals; by the eighties, there were more than a hundred unofficial magazines. (At the same time, there were only five official magazines dealing with culture.)

Samizdat literature was only one of the ways in which the repressed culture expressed itself. There were seminars in philosophy, and lecture series were held on different areas of the humanities. Young people frequently tried to distance themselves entirely from the pseudo-culture offered to them by the authorities. They founded small theatres, and from the seventies on, the most authentic expression of their relationship to the ruling system was the protest song. Singers who were closest to them in age and attitude became their idols. The authorities reacted predictably, and one generation of protest singers was essentially driven into exile, but as usual, the results were the opposite of what was intended.

By the late eighties, the international situation was undoubtedly influential. Those who represented power and those who represented culture were clearly squared off against each other. Several events also sharpened the conflict between the authorities and those who were trying to extricate themselves from their toils. The authorities frequently used police brutality to break up memorial assemblies to commemorate the country's national holiday or the memory of Jan Palach, a student who had set fire to himself, and died, in protest against the Soviet invasion. Those who came to pay their respects to a person who symbolized the possibility of individual protest taken to its furthest extreme became the object of a violent attack by special units who used truncheons, water-cannons and tear-gas. People, mostly the young, decided not to give way to violence. For five consecutive days the peaceful assemblies were repeated, and on four occasions the police used violence to break them up. Several people were arrested, Václav Havel among them. During these events, which aroused the emotions of the whole country, the cruel truth about power was publicly revealed for the first time. At this critical juncture, the government could not find a single person with sufficient authority to address the nation. No one was willing to give public support to the regime, but many could be found to protest against police brutality, against imprisoning the innocent. Among the protesters were actors, filmmakers and writers who, until then, the regime had believed to be on 'its side'.

In this critical situation, the authorities—and it is hard to say whether this was out of stupidity or desperation or arrogance, or the awareness that they were indeed indelibly tarnished—refused all invitations by the cultural opposition to take part in a dialogue. The deep chasm between totalitarian power and all the 'shaken', to use Patočka's term, became unbridgeable. It was clear that any further error, any further act of arrogance, might be fatal.

What happened in November 1989 is well known. As an eyewitness and a participant, I wish to emphasize that this revolution, which really was the outcome of a clash between culture and power, was the most non-violent revolution imaginable. In the mass meetings attended by up to three-quarters of a million people, no one was hurt, not a window was broken, not a car damaged. Many of the tens of thousands of pamphlets that flooded Prague and other cities and towns urged people to peaceful, tolerant action; not one called for violence. For those who still believe in the power of culture, the power of words, of good and of love, and their dominance over violence, who believe that neither the poet nor Archimedes, in their struggle against the man in uniform, are beaten before they begin, the Prague revolution must have been an inspiration.

Abridged from a paper delivered at a symposium held by the Praemium Erasmianum in the Hague, May 1990

THE BEGINNING AND THE END
OF TOTALITARIANISM

As THE REVOLUTIONARY events that led to a renewal of the demo-cratic system in Czechoslovakia in 1989 were unfolding, I became aware of an almost incredible resemblance to the *coup d'état* that led to the establishment of a totalitarian Communist regime in 1948. In neither case were there bloody confronta-tions; the fate of the country was decided in the public squares of the capital city where huge demonstrations in 1948 demanded an end to democracy, and, forty years later, called for an end to totalitarianism. In both cases, one of the decisive moments of the overthrow was the behaviour of the media. In 1948, the typesetters refused to set type for the democratic newspapers, the Communists occupied the radio station (televi-sion did not yet exist) and, as a result, were the only ones capable of influencing public opinion in the decisive moments. In 1989, a turning-point came when staff at the television station announced that they would stop broadcasting if they were not allowed to inform the public truthfully about the course of events. Even the typesetters of the Communist daily threatened to strike if their paper did not print the truth about the unfolding events. In both cases, the existing governments collapsed in a few days.

The demise of totalitarian regimes of the left and of the right over the past few decades might lead us to the erroneous and optimistic conclusion that these regimes were somehow alien to the very essence of human behaviour and thinking, that they came into being merely through some oversight of history.

In reality, many people unconsciously long for the kind of order and firm-handed government they promised. I have recalled the enthusiasm with which the totalitarian system was established in my country forty years ago, and I still remember the wild excitement that greeted Hitler's accession to power in Germany. The first half of our century demonstrated that totalitarian systems attracted whole societies, entire nations. They achieved their popularity through a combination of utopian visions and demagogic promises, and also by appealing to the ideas the average citizens had about order and a just organization of society. To people trapped in the greyness of everyday life, they offered a great ideal, as well as a charismatic leader who relieved them of the burden of having to decide for themselves, of responsibility and risk, and, moreover, led them towards a goal that gave their lives a meaning. Many aspects of a totalitarian system in its early stages are impressive: its decisiveness, the clarity of its programme, and the energy with which it deals with problems that a democracy, by its very nature, cannot solve in that way. It bans what upsets the average citizen and takes measures that impress him. The regime metes out a portion of what it confiscated or stole during its rise to power; it frightens, locks up or kills those who disagree with it and thus it creates the appearance of unity. At first it seems almost magically effective, and it reinforces this impact with magnificent and ostentatious celebrations, demonstrations and parades. In its early days, the totalitarian regime seems strong precisely because of the mass support it enjoys and the unity, at least on the surface, that it demonstrates.

What happened over the course of one or two generations to cause this regime to collapse? Why did its children and grandchildren long to return to the old democracy that their forebears had so demonstrably and enthusiastically abandoned?

A totalitarian regime must constantly recreate unity, for this, after all, is its essence. Both ideologically and in the civic sense, this unity is symbolized by the Leader—the founder, the discoverer, the unifier. He embodies not only the totalitarian ideal, but the movement that brought the idea to life. In the first phase, because of the personality of the leader and his cohorts (it was they who were able to sway the citizen and then confidently, and usually with great determination, carry through their notions of social order), the totalitarian system appears to be dynamic, a system that has overturned the old order, its laws, customs and traditions. But the very principle of totalitarianism assumes that everyone will submit, that everyone will unite in the name of the idea, the leader, the centre of power.

Every totalitarian system thus aims at both the elimination of personality (except for the personality of the leader, whether embodied in a single human being or in a group), and at the elevation of impersonality, that is, of people who, regardless of how diligent, industrious or thorough they are, deliberately repress in themselves every germ of individuality and initiative. What at first appeared to be a dynamic system, becomes heavy-handed, clumsy and sluggish. A totalitarian system favours and promotes a single individual or group at the expense of all others, so it must necessarily come into conflict not only with the needs of many individuals, but also with those of the entire community. In modern society especially, not even the most brilliant individual or the best organized centre of power can prevent problems from piling up. After the first apparent outburst of success, every totalitarian society enters a period of crisis that affects almost every aspect of life. It is reflected first in the intellectual sphere; totalitarian power does not allow differing opinions and therefore does not allow debate or even meaningful conversation. Intellectual activity is impossible. Every individual, regardless of his inner make-up, has to adapt to the official model; the development of his personality is restrained; the space in which the human mind and spirit moves becomes continually narrower.

Those who try to defend themselves against such a development increase in number; they protest and demand change. The totalitarian system knows only one response. It uses force against the discontented. This is why totalitarian states cannot exist without political police, compliant courts, illegal sentencing, concentration camps and executions that are often just crudely disguised murders. Although at the outset many are horrified by these actions, they are eventually persuaded that such methods are at least effective. Indeed, at the peak of its evolution, the totalitarian system is remarkable for the number of obedient servants it can deploy throughout society. They are different from the initial supporters, however, in that they serve the regime for different reasons. They are no longer moved by enthusiasm, but by fear.

Yet the person whose actions are motivated by constant fear loses a quality from which our entire culture grew: he loses creativity, he loses perspective. His behaviour can be likened to that of the inhabitant of a city under siege. His sole desire is to survive.

Once the number of apparently loyal citizens, those obedient but uncreative servants, reaches its peak, when the results of the elections are overwhelmingly in favour of the regime, then, paradoxically, the regime begins to crack. Because of its slowness to respond, this crisis quickly spreads from the intellectual and spiritual sphere to all other spheres of life. It grips the economy, human relationships and morality, and is ultimately reflected even in matters such as the pollution of the water and the air, for which no one takes responsibility. Totalitarian power usually denies that there is a crisis and attempts to turn it to its own advantage. That is, it tries to transform into a privilege everything that, until recently, was a normal human need, but which, thanks to totalitarianism, has become a rarity. Then it bribes its citizens: the right to a roof over your head becomes a privilege, along with the right to uncontaminated food, medical care, uncensored information, permission to travel, education, warmth and, finally, to life itself.

Because the regime turns everything into a privilege, everything becomes a means of corrupting people. The regime batters people's civic awareness and their self-confidence. Depending on how deep the crisis is and how advanced the decay of society, the *nomenklatura*, the stratum of people who enjoy exceptional privileges, is broad. Members of the *nomenklatura* are then placed beyond criticism and above the law. They can do things others cannot, even commit crimes. The privileged caste quickly becomes demoralized and changes into a stratum of corrupt, fat and incompetent servants of the system. But because the regime provides them with power and entrusts most of the important functions and offices to them, they are precisely the ones who contribute most to the deepening of the social crisis, and to the ever more obvious incapacity of the totalitarian regime.

Typically, the *nomenklatura* is incapable of producing from within its ranks an outstanding or charismatic personality. If the regime survives the death of its leader or the generation of its original leaders, the government passes into the hands of nonentities who quickly lead society into a deep decline. We observed the same phenomenon in almost all the countries of Eastern and Central Europe: they were governed by people so dull that not only were they unable to do anything to save the system to which they owed everything, but they had nothing to offer the society they were governing, and thus they had no other influence except raw power.

The totalitarian system comes to power by promising to improve society and the lives of its citizens. It loses power by destroying the way society is organized, and thus worsening the lives of most of the population. The end of totalitarian regimes—whether of the left or of the right—comes about in various ways, sometimes bloodily, sometimes surprisingly swiftly and peacefully. Sometimes they are swept away in a popular uprising; at other times their end is the outcome of the work of reformers who appear from inside the system at a time when the regimes have obviously lost all means of keeping society functioning even on a basic level. There has not been a single totalitarian system with any real vitality that has not condemned its citizens to greater physical and mental hardship than the democratic societies. By allowing an unlimited and unshakeable government by a single individual (who was often morally and mentally deranged), totalitarianism is a disaster not only for those it governs, but for all humanity. In the recent past, particularly in times of crisis, totalitarian government represented a choice that seemed to large segments of society to make sense. When today's gloomy experiences have been half forgotten, or when society finds itself in deep crisis, they may once again present to people a dangerously attractive alternative.

1990

CZECHOSLOVAKIA: A PREMATURE
OBITUARY

WHEN IT FINALLY died, the Czechoslovak Republic had not
attained an age much beyond the average life expectancy of
women in our part of the world. Because such an age is still
childhood in the life of a country, we can say that the republic,
afflicted by many diseases, died prematurely. Rather than
making it tough and resilient by building up immunities, the
diseases undermined its strength long-term.

Even so, the collapse of the country surprised many Czechs
and Slovaks. Until recently, according to polls, more than eighty
per cent of the citizens in both republics favoured keeping the
country together. Those who were surprised will probably agree
about one thing: the impulse towards separation came from
Slovakia, and insofar as the Czechs contributed to it, it was
mainly by having refused, for so long, to take the Slovak separatists or, more precisely, Slovak desires for greater autonomy,
seriously. In the elections of June 1992, Slovak parties with a
separatist platform of one kind or another received almost
eighty per cent of the vote. (There were no such parties in the
Czech republic.) Many supporters of a common Czecho-Slovak
state claim that in the elections, the Slovaks fell victim to their
own ignorance by not realizing that while the transformation of
the common state into a confederation, as the winning party in
Slovakia proposed in its programme, assumed willingness on
both sides, the idea of a confederation had no support in the
Czech lands. But such an explanation is unsatisfactory. Closer to
the truth is the observation that the Slovak voters wanted some-

thing unattainable: a completely independent state that would, at the same time, maintain the advantages of coexistence in the larger whole, the advantages of the common state.

*

Czechoslovakia was created in 1918, not only as a political entity—a country—but also as a word. In the past, the Czechs and Slovaks were linked mainly by the nearness of their languages. (On the territory inhabited by the Slavs there were, until recently, many dialects that subtly linked the individual languages: moving east, Czech gradually blended into Slovak, Slovak into Ruthenian, Ruthenian into Ukrainian and so on. There were fewer differences between the Czech spoken in Eastern Moravia and the Slovak of the adjacent Western Slovakia than there were between the Slovak of Western and Eastern Slovakia.)

Nevertheless, contact between the Czechs and Slovaks over the centuries had been infrequent, and their histories were different. The Czech kingdom had been an independent state and as such played an important role in Central European history between the thirteenth and the seventeenth centuries. The same could not be said of the people of the Upper Hungarian kingdom who lived under the rule of Pest. The borders of any eventual Slovak state were not even defined. Relations between Prague and Pest varied, but they never amounted to much. There was very little in the awareness of either Slavic entity that could have united them. It was only in the last century, during the period of national revival movements, that the Slovak 'awakeners'—the scholars, writers and linguists who attempted to resist the harsh Hungarianization policies—began to look to the Czechs for support, since the Czechs were closest to them linguistically and had already achieved some success in resisting Germanization. Thus originated the image of the Czechs as the older, more experienced Slavic brother from whom the Slovaks sought advice, support and protection. The ideal, the goal of the nationalist efforts at that time, however, was nothing like a common country; it was simply more cultural and linguistic autonomy within the framework of the Austro-Hungarian Empire.

*

Even when the First World War was reaching its climax, the idea of a common state of Czechs and Slovaks was almost unheard-of at home. It had emerged, mainly in the United States, in the final years of the war, just as the unrealistic and rather utilitarian idea of a single Czechoslovak nation was worked out there. When the war was over, these ideas were supported by the victorious powers as part of their policy to weaken the defeated Austro-Hungarian Empire. To the new republic of Czechoslovakia were added the Hungarian regions adjacent to the north banks of the Danube and the Ipel, and the territory of Ruthenia at the extreme eastern end of Slovakia. The latter was a world away from Prague linguistically and culturally, and in its economic backwardness it was far behind even the industrially undeveloped Slovakia. The merging of these three entities into a single state created problems precisely because of the vast cultural and economic gaps between them. While the Czech lands inherited from the Habsburg empire the major share of a productive and modern industrial base, Slovakia entered the new republic as a backward agricultural region with virtually no intelligentsia of its own. Paradoxically, the first teachers of the Slovak language in Slovak schools came from the Czech lands, as did most of the doctors, specialists and civil servants.

At the moment of its birth, however, the republic was cel-ebrated with exaggerated hopes. People cried with joy, sang patriotic songs, tore down the emblems and trappings of the former regime and cheered at rallies. Czechs and Slovaks brimmed with fraternal feeling. The newly independent state appeared to make possible a completely different, free spiritual and intellectual development, and above all, to put the destiny of the nation (they spoke of themselves as a single nation) in its own hands. It also seemed that the new state had been born under optimum circumstances. Its potential enemies were disabled: the great power to the west—Germany—had lost the war, the former Austro-Hungarian monarchy was not only dead, but had been posthumously divided, and the great power to the east—Russia—was torn by revolutionary confusion. Moreover, the new Czechoslovak republic enjoyed a favourable status with the victorious powers.

Some of the dreams of those who celebrated the birth of the new state were fulfilled. The country developed culturally and created a relatively well-functioning democratic system inspired chiefly by the constitution of France. Nevertheless, it soon became clear that their other hopes were unfounded. Both Germany and Russia recovered from their wounds with remarkable alacrity and soon began to interfere dangerously in the internal affairs of the young country. This interference was made easier by the complexity of the situation in matters of social and ethnic policy, where the new republic was incapable of dealing with growing tensions.

*

In the eyes of the world, there has long existed the idea of Czechoslovakia as a unified and essentially prosperous country, particularly compared with most of the countries around it. This view from the outside, however, did not take into account all the inner tensions, all the ups and downs and difficulties of co-existence.

In reality, there were few periods during the seventy-four years of Czechoslovakia's existence that could be called peaceful or even happy. At the very beginning of the country's life, Slovakia was afflicted by a major political and economic crisis (a large part of Slovakia was occupied for a time by the Hungarian Red Army), and after a brief period of prosperity the whole country was hit by the great economic depression of the thirties (once again, the impact on Slovakia and Ruthenia was worse). During the country's twenty years of independent existence between the wars, ethnic tension increased in Czechoslovakia: tension between the Czechs and Slovaks on the one hand, and the many minorities (mainly the German and the Hungarian) on the other, and between the Czechs and the Slovaks themselves. The problems of Czecho-Slovak relations had their origins in both economics and culture. Thanks to their history and geographical position, the Czechs had entered the union as the stronger partner. While the Slovaks could boast no personalities of worldwide significance, the Czechs had their Jan Hus, and their Komenský (or Comenius, as he is known elsewhere, and who, like Masaryk after him, was born not far from the present border with Slovakia), their Dvořák, Smetana,

Janáček, Hašek and Čapek. They had one of the oldest Middle-European universities, and in the past famous kings and emperors had ruled over vast kingdoms from Prague. Prague itself was not only the capital of the republic, but was considered one of the traditional centres of European learning. The Czechs had conquered illiteracy in the last century and their schools had produced many who went on to gain world reputations in their fields.

The Slovaks, on the other hand, were just starting off in all fields, and suffered from feelings of inferiority. Many Czechs looked down their noses at them. While a knowledge of Czech culture was considered essential among educated Slovaks, there was, with few exceptions, no similar interest in Slovakia on the part of the Czechs. The Czech sense of superiority was reflected in practically every sphere of life. It isn't surprising, then, that the Czechs considered the republic as their own, while the relationship of many Slovaks to the republic was not nearly as straightforward. What first appeared to the Slovaks as friendly assistance soon became, in the eyes of many, a rather unpleasant form of patronage, and unfair competition for the newly emerging Slovak intelligentsia, bureaucracy, or entrepreneurial class. It was not long after the initial euphoria over their newly won freedom that the first signs of nationalism and separatist tendencies began to appear in Slovakia, and these intensified from year to year, becoming an explicit desire for a country that Slovaks could truly consider theirs, and theirs alone.

The first stage of Czechoslovak history ended tragically. The day before the Nazi invasion and occupation of the Czech lands, an independent Slovak state (under the patronage of Hitler, and with parts of it ceded to Hungary) was declared. (The Czechs rightly felt this Slovak move as a stab in the back in their most difficult hour.) The Republic died on 15 March 1939. The new Slovak state, administered by a quasi-fascist government (which even sent an army unit to fight alongside Hitler's troops on the eastern front), made it possible for most Slovaks (with the exception of the Jews, of course) to survive the war with far fewer hardships than people in the Czech lands had to undergo.

At the same time, it must be emphasized that where forces assembled against Hitler abroad, Czechs and Slovaks also fought together against the Axis powers. And, in the summer of 1944 in Slovakia, a relatively widespread popular uprising against the collaborationist regime took place.

After the war, the Czechoslovak republic was renewed, and its rebirth was accompanied by public enthusiasm comparable to the enthusiasm with which both Czechs and Slovaks had welcomed its inception in 1918. Yet the mutual relations between the Czechs and the Slovaks were still not satisfactorily resolved. The Slovaks were given a few unremarkable concessions by the Czech side: a government of their own, but one appointed by the government in Prague. For the next four decades little could change: the whole country became a vassal of the Soviet Union, which had an interest in maintaining a strict status quo in the strategically important area close to its western borders. In the brief liberal period of the Prague Spring, the Slovaks managed to push through a federal constitution for the Czechoslovak state. It theoretically guaranteed them a number of rights, and gave them not only their own parliament and government, but established a second chamber in the federal parliament in which both nations had the same number of seats and each was given a collective veto over the other. Naturally, under the communist government, the parliaments always voted unanimously in response to directives issued by the central party organs or by Moscow, not in the interests of their own voters. After the Soviet occupation, Moscow deliberately used the Slovak Communists to suppress the rebellious Czechs. For the first time in the country's history, there were Slovaks in the highest, or at least the most influential, positions, and the Czechs unjustifiably suspected them of using their positions to arrange the transfer of considerable material resources from the Czech lands to Slovakia, bringing relative prosperity to Slovakia at the price of devastation of the Czech environment and a deepening deterioration of Czech industry.

The coexistence of the Czechs and Slovaks, as a consequence of external circumstances as much as internal ones, brought problems with it that could not, in the eyes of Slovak politicians, be immediately resolved, and these cancelled out the achievements of those seventy years when the two nations did, in fact, grow closer together in all areas of life.

•

Despite all the negative things that have transpired between the Czechs and Slovaks, there is little that is rational about the breakup of the country. During those seventy years of common life many differences were overcome, and the new democratic conditions after 1989 gave Slovaks real autonomy for the first time within the federal framework. It would seem to go against all logic that the weaker of the two partners, Slovakia, would be the one to push for separation. Given its geographical position, it risks having the rest of Europe lump it together with the Balkans. If it gives some sober thought to its future, it must fear for the security of its borders. And it has an unemployment rate three times higher than the Czech lands. Yet the separation will certainly weaken the position of both countries in Europe, which at this time is far from being stable, and whose own future is unpredictable.

Nationalism, however, is seldom rational. It often treats a desire as though it were a reality, and exaggerates both its own potential and the damage done to it by its alleged rival. As I write this, the separation seems irreversible. This is certainly due to the outcome of the elections. In the Czech lands, the right-wing democratic forces won the elections; in Slovakia, the winners were a coalition of nationalists and left-oriented separatists whose behaviour since the elections fills democrats with foreboding about the future of democracy and economic reform in an independent Slovakia.

The Czech and the Slovak sides have both, for different reasons, an interest in a quick separation. The Czech side fears for the future of their economic reforms, which the socialistic tendencies of the Slovak side could thwart. The Slovak separatists are in a hurry to realize their vision of an independent Slovakia while the wave of nationalism is still sweeping this part of Europe and they can still project their actions into a wider and apparently justified movement. Nevertheless both sides, though they must constantly overcome mutual distrust and refute often unfounded slurs, are trying to bring off a civilized separation. Reason, after all, suggests that any excesses of the

Yugoslav type would mean the end of dreams of returning to Europe. Even though reason is seldom heeded in such cases, another indication that the separation will be peaceful is that the Czechs and Slovaks have never fought against each other and that in general (and this is especially true of Czechs) it is not their habit to settle things by violence.

> *October 1992. Written for 'Svenska Dagbladet'.*
> *Expanded for this collection*

IV

ON THE LITERATURE OF SECULAR FAITH

EVER SINCE MAN became aware of his own being, he has known of death. Man comes and goes, while the world, life and time remain. In the history of culture, we may observe how people have come to terms with the inevitable paradox of life and the question—given that paradox—of the meaning of human life.

However eastern and western cultures may differ in their notions of God and the significance of human actions, we sense that at the beginning they must have asked a similar question: how do we best spend the time allotted to us? How do we come to terms with our own mortality? How do we transcend it? Face to face with nature, where everything is constantly coming into being and perishing, man longed to find something lasting, something that would defy extinction, something or someone he could relate to, in which he could find assurances of some kind of permanence.

The more man separated himself from nature and the more he began to differ from other mortal creatures, the more he realized that the one who is above the world of the living had granted him a special beneficence. Man was chosen, created in His image. Yet how could one who had shown man such beneficence have, at the same time, so repudiated him as to have made him like the other creatures and granted him no more than a tiny island in the sea of time? Man sensed that some small reflection, at least, of divine greatness and immortality had taken root in him. He sensed that he had a soul, and that the soul did not succumb to death along with the body. It was immortal, or, at least, it sought to achieve heights where it would once more

131

reunite with God, from whom it emanated.

But this hope was not completely satisfying either, and so he finally accepted the most comforting news of all: that the Son of God had conquered death by His sacrifice on the cross. Today Christians still utter the credo: I believe in the resurrection of the body. Man may enter eternity not only with his soul, but with his body. If the disciples of Jesus had promised no more than this, they would still have found throngs of supporters, people willing to live and die for the new creed.

Yet even with the comfort the gospel of life's triumph over death provided, there remained the depressing separation of the world of the dead from the world of the living, of heaven from earth, of people from God. We have no word from the other side. Reason, the questioner, questions the logic of this separation and begins to doubt. But it elicits the response: if you don't wish to die, believe! Your faith will save you. Only through faith can man be liberated from the kingdom of non-being.

Man is distinguished from other living beings by his awareness of himself, by his reason, by his ability to ask questions and to map the connections between things, causes, laws of nature. In matters of faith, however, he enters a kingdom where he must remind himself not to ask questions, just to believe, for fear he die. The more reason reveals to us the mysteries of the material world, the more the dualism of reason and faith deepens and strengthens.

I don't feel competent to say anything about the essence of the debate that reason and faith have had with each other since time immemorial, but I think I can fairly say that in the last two centuries, the number of people who find aspects of church dogma unacceptable has increased. Those brought up in an atmosphere of rationalism—the children of the technical or the atomic age—tend to recoil when they hear that old creed about the resurrection of the body at the end of time. Even those who long to believe are often unable to do so with the same intensity as their forefathers; instead of a comforting faith, they experience fear of nothingness. A century and a half ago, the poet Karel Hynek Macha brilliantly expressed the emotions of someone confronted by a universe without God:

A star dipped from the heaven's heights
A dead star, an azure light.
It falls in a kingdom without end,
It falls eternally in eternal existence.
Its weeping echoes from the grave of all things,
A terrible howl, a frightful wail
'When will the end of my existence come?'
Never—nowhere—there is no goal.

But can man live in fear of nothingness? He must, after all, find some meaning in his actions, a purpose for his life, even if he refuses to seek it where his ancestors have found it for centuries. The time now favours prophets of new faiths. Crowds listen to them and follow them. The longing to believe in meaning and salvation persists; only the direction and the object of cults is changing. Faith descends from heaven to earth, from life after death to life in this world, where man, not God, is worshipped. Increasingly, it is only man as a symbol, embodied in the figure of the great leader.

The writer in modern times, too, is often unwilling or unable to accept a faith that brought his predecessors salvation. He may, however, repeat as often as he wants: *Exegi menumentum aere perennius* ('I have completed a monument more lasting than bronze'), but he cannot get around the basic paradox of his own being and non-being. And what hope has he to offer people?

At the same time, many writers feel like latter-day prophets. They long to have the prophet's sense of urgency and drama, and they try, as the prophets did, to warn and point to the higher way. But the one who dispatched the prophets in the first place is missing.

The last century unleashed a mighty outpouring of prophetic literature. Writers such as Dickens, Zola and Hugo all viewed the world in a similar way. Human society is unjust, the world is by and large a gloomy place, and authors are most interested in areas where social dramas, or more precisely tragedies, are enacted, where either the poverty and suffering brought about by social inequality or the cynical, corrupting power of money, dominates. This prophetic wrath over the misery of human affairs has its literary proponents even today,

133

but there was always something missing: a rock from which the prophet could speak. For in whose name was he actually preaching? And what was he preaching? What was he offering? He knew that poverty was terrible, and he claimed that richness spoiled people. But the life of a person who acknowledges no higher power can only oscillate between the two alternatives.

The audience—an appropriate word to describe them, I think—to whom these secular prophets spoke, were primed for a liberating message. Could it be entirely disregarded? Everything was ripe for the acceptance of any doctrine that offered salvation. The age of the grand ideologies had begun.

All the ideologies that had so fatal an influence on events in the first half of the twentieth century were born deep in the nineteenth. It was only the general need, the growing hunger for a redemptive doctrine, that lent them an air of universality and made them seem more important even than human lives. The one that had the greatest impact on human destiny was Marx's theory of scientific socialism, a just social order that the working class would create after a victorious revolution.

In the new post-revolutionary society man would no longer exploit man. Technology, which would serve human welfare, would eliminate the need for drudgery. Society's wealth would be distributed according to merit, and unearned income would vanish along with the poverty of working people. Gradually, as the social wealth increased, everyone would be rewarded according to his needs. Ultimately, the state, money and private property would wither away; the alienation of man from his work and from himself would be no more. Paradise would descend on earth.

At last, all who longed to be prophets now had a word that they could use, as their predecessors had done, to cast a spell over the masses: Socialism!

Authors who accepted the new doctrine brought into literature new themes and settings, and a non-traditional hero—a self-confident, determined figure from a humble (usually working-class) background. (The prototype of such literature is found in the work of Maxim Gorky, particularly his book *Mother*.) Socialist writers also pointed out the cruel conditions in which large numbers lived, and on their behalf, prophesied the destruction of the existing social order and the advent of a new and more humane order. For—what a relief!—the socialist writer possessed, or believed he possessed, a material from which he could create his own kingdom of heaven, his own myth of salvation.

The new myth, oddly, retained many aspects of the old faith. It had a chosen people and a promised land, and leaders to take them there. It even had its own minor deities, its golden calves, its heretics, who had to be exposed and destroyed. But because this myth was mundane, because this literature, in the words of Albert Camus, substituted 'idealistic aims for real aims, and sought the meaning of human life in how man fulfilled these aims,' it contained within itself a danger: the faith it required was even more open to abuse than the faith it was trying to supplant.

The place in which man actually lived was always kept separate from the realm of the ideal, whether it was called paradise or the kingdom of heaven. That separation, however, did not subvert the real world, the one man lived in. Now, however, the socialist vision presupposed that the ideal world would actually be created on this earth. It would rise on the ruins of the old society. Unlike the societies that had come before it, and that had evolved spontaneously, this new society was to be the outcome of planning by socialist 'architects'. But at the very heart of the revolutionary vision of the ideal society lay hidden the idea of disjunction, the denial or at least the discrediting of values, institutions and experiences that humanity has spent centuries evolving.

The old notion of a chosen people was also revived in the populist illusion about the simple man who carries the truth about with him and is a well-spring of wisdom and uncorrupted morality, and was transformed into the myth of the historical mission of the working class.

Every such abstraction in literature—an abstraction in which truth and good are known in advance, and the moral qualities of a man are derived from his origins, whether his race, nation or class—is deadly. The near future would show us what kind of impact this would have on life.

Eventually—aided by a pointless world war—the proletarian

revolution was victorious on one-sixth of the earth's surface. The first socialist state was born, and the vision of countless socialist prophets was fulfilled. A redemptive hope once again descended among the people.

Thus the ancient couple, reason and faith, were with us once more. But they differed in essential ways from the traditional couple. The new object of worship was an outcome of the same reason that rejected faith, that is, faith in someone who stands above the world. Reason worshipped its own creation, its most rational work, and it offered it to people as a new source of hope. The distance between finiteness and eternity, between the human and the divine, between eternal non-being and immortality, between the body and the soul, vanished. Hope lost its metaphysical dimension. Hope in a better organized world remained, but can human affairs really be better organized when the metaphysical dimension is missing?

From the moment the word became flesh, socialist faith and socialist literature took on a new dimension. The dreams and visions of prophets and their audiences suddenly began to be made real, and the results could be measured.

With the distance of many years, much of what the revolution contributed or perpetrated appears differently to us from the way it did to contemporaries. It is beyond dispute that each revolution brings its supporters an intoxicating satisfaction, a feeling that they are not the playthings of history, but its creators and even its ameliorators, in the name of great, pure ideals that promise to lead humanity out of misery. The feelings of revolutionary leaders may be compared with the feelings of apostles of salvation. In the words of Malraux: 'In the life of the revolutionary, revolution plays the same role that eternal life once played. It brings salvation to those who make it.'

The writer is, moreover, offered the hope that the socialist revolutionary will eliminate all the laws and conventions of the pre-revolutionary society that bound him, and the hope of entering an empire of unlimited freedom. He also believes that society will pay more attention to him because, as the theory goes, the revolution will provide unprecedented opportunities for culture, and therefore for literature. They will cease to be a marginal matters of interest to only a handful, and will belong to all the people, be needed by all the people. In socialism, after all, in Trotsky's delirious vision: 'The average man can become an Aristotle, a Goethe, a Marx.'

Is it any wonder that many writers believed that destiny had made them participants in the most revolutionary events in modern history? This feeling was reflected in the first works of socialist literature, and it would be unjust to make light of them. Mayakovsky, Babel and John Reed or Mikhail Sholokhov, author of *And Quiet Flows the Don*, undoubtedly produced testimonies to their own feelings and those of the people who made the revolution.

But the time came when the individuals who led the revolution and fed the crowds with promises had to render an account of their activity, and when they did, they found they had little to show for it. They could only encourage people to be patient, to be firm in the faith—and excommunicate those who refused to submit.

The temptations of the Great Saving Hope, however, remained. The revolution, after all, was trying to realize its faith under siege. Such grand ideas must be given more time. Most writers, who found in the socialist revolution the expression of their ideals, their hopes and the hopes of all people, did not abandon the ranks of the faithful prophets. Among them are recognized artists like Barbusse, Brecht, Rolland, Laxness or Nexø. They saw nothing—but believed. And they didn't want anyone else to see for himself, they merely wanted everyone to share their faith. *In the Land Where Tomorrow Means Yesterday* was what one Czech author called an anthology of fulsome reports on the Soviet Union. The faithful prophet enthusiastically spouts slogans about the new justice, is ecstatic about the new tractor factories, about the comradely relationships. He finds himself in a land where dreams are being transformed into realities. But of the hundreds of thousands of innocent people who have been dragged off to Siberian concentration camps, he knows nothing. The Russian author Maxim Gorky went even further. Officials invited him to inspect a concentration camp on the Solovetskiye Islands. He accepted, and wrote an enthusiastic sketch of his visit. Through his eyes, the concentration camp becomes a re-educational institution where they employ 'educational working methods in conditions of the greatest freedom'. Nothing looks like a prison. It is a place where people are educating themselves and learning to live in a civilized manner, performing plays, raising sables, foxes, cows and pigs. 'For the first time, I saw horse and cow stables kept in a state of such cleanliness that the sharp stench usually emanating from such places cannot be detected at all.' On the other hand he discovers, to his distaste, that there are political prisoners among the inmates—'counter-revolutionaries of the emotional type, monarchists, those who before the revolution were called the Black Hundreds. There are exponents of terrorism, economic spies, and all the weeds that the just hand of history has plucked out of the field.'

He was also moved by the beauty of the setting. 'The rough lyricism of these islands, without evoking a sterile sympathy for its inhabitants, awakens an almost torturous longing to work more rapidly and fervently towards creating a new reality . . . ' For the new reality, as every prophet true to his faith knows, will no longer need prisons, not even these wonderful, free re-education camps. 'In the Union of Socialist Soviet Republics, it is recognized that crime is a product of class society, that crime is a social disease festering in the rotten soil of private ownership, and that it will be wiped out if we wipe out the conditions that created the disease in the first place—the ancient, rotting economic foundations of the class society . . . '

According to a claim later made by Alexander Solzhenitsyn, a fourteen-year-old prisoner told Gorky, during his visit, about the horrors of camp life. 'Gorky left the barracks and wept . . . As soon as his steamship had left, they shot the boy.' If such an encounter did take place, the prophet remained silent. He could not, after all, spoil his prophetic portrait of paradise. But his behaviour became the model for how to write about the socialist reality. He demonstrated how the socialist writer should look at the life he is shown, or more precisely, should look *exclusively* at the life he is shown, and see it only the way it is shown to him.

We must refine Camus's description of socialist literature: socialist literature seeks the meaning of life in how man realizes the goals of the ruling political force in the country of the revolution, and in how his activity and his attitudes help this power reinforce its rule.

It was not only writers from the land of revolution who could and did contribute to this: writers came from abroad as well. The writer was asked to accept that the aim of the existing power in the land of the revolution was to build as quickly as possible first a socialist and then a communist society, which would go on to realize all its original ideals. In other words, everyone will, in the end, attain freedom and material well-being. But, the argument went, that power had run up against fierce resistance both internationally and from its own domestic reactionaries, and therefore had to take extraordinary measures. Such measures, however, were not typical of socialism, and thus no attention should be paid to them. We were compelled to take them by external circumstances, and they would disappear when the circumstances went away. On the contrary, it was advisable to call on the creative power in the people, their enthusiasm, their success in building socialism. The more the people came under the yoke of violence, the more the prophets are expected to celebrate them.

'The main heroes of our literature are people building a new life, the workers, the collective farmers, men and women, party members, economic experts, engineers, members of the Komsomol, the Young Pioneers. Our literature is vibrant with enthusiasm and heroism . . . It is essentially optimistic, for it is literature of the class that is on the rise—the proletariat, the one progressive and pioneering class . . . Soviet literature must be able to present our heroes and look into our tomorrows. This will not be a utopia, for our future has been prepared in a planned way, through correct political work today.' Thus spake A. A. Zhdanov, addressing the first All-Union Writers' Congress in 1934. And at the same conference, Gorky formulated an incontrovertible law:

'Genuine literature, genuine truth, is to be found in heroes of the people, in those ancient and eternal heroes of the working people such as Prometheus, Svayatogor, Ivanushka, Petrushka and, ultimately, in Lenin.'

This challenge was issued at a time when the eyes of the prophets, instead of looking through the gates of heaven, were

139

most frequently looking though the gates of prison, where they could scarcely fail to hear the cries of the innocent. For that was how it was—the desperate and tortured prisoners confessed to unbelievable crimes, famine was raging in territories until not long before thought to be the breadbasket of Europe, people—the known and unknown, believers and unbelievers, revolutionaries and their opponents—were disappearing from their homes, many never to be seen again. The dead bodies piled up; books about this appeared abroad; there were witnesses enough willing to testify. Yet those who, until recently, had felt an antipathy to every lawless act, who cried for help on behalf of all those who suffered, suddenly knew nothing about any of this.

Naturally, when the conflict between the ideal and reality increases, heretics and critics appear who are able to attract many followers. The faith must be defended steadfastly and ruthlessly against them, as befits the only scientifically based truth about society.

In 1936, after returning from the land of the revolution, one of the newer prophets, André Gide, published a book of reportage called *Retour de l'URSS*, in which he admitted to disappointments and second thoughts. The book outraged true believers. In Czechoslovakia too, S. K. Neumann, a not entirely insignificant poet, wrote a book in response called *Anti-Gide*, in which he heaps insult and ridicule on the French writer. In doing so he created a catechism that summarized the dogma of socialist faith. It is interesting to compare Neumann's confession of faith with earlier utopian visions. The huge gap is obvious in the very language he uses: pathos is replaced by paroxysm, visions of the future give way to lies about the present and angry tirades against opponents and backsliders, against Christians, democrats, Trotskyites, revisionists, intellectuals, members of the intelligentsia, the petty bourgeoisie, liberals, individualists, surrealists, decadents and leeches drown out all the rest of the positive message. One unshakeable hope remains: 'The Soviet Union is the only security in the world of today.'

The revolution once attracted great spirits to its cause by promising to liberate man. Now, suddenly, the alleged defender of its heritage is declaring a notion of socialist freedom that has more in common with standing orders in a military barracks or a prison than it does with the recent visions.

'Socialism cannot allow anyone to say whatever comes into his head. It cannot allow anyone to slap together a party and an organization around just anything. Socialism is a plan and an order that must be observed by everyone. Socialism is not free competition . . . it cannot support individualism in production, nor in any of the elements of the superstructure. Socialism recognizes only the personality that understands the meaning and the necessity of having everyone adhere to the plan, and that actually adheres to it. Socialism rejects individualistic, arbitrary acts; it needs disciplined individuals and disciplined individualities. Socialism is not bourgeois freedom, socialism is not liberalism, socialism is discipline.'

The author of these lines had begun his career as a decadent poet and an anarchist and was the first to publish, in his own magazine, in Czech, the as yet-unknown author Franz Kafka. Yet with even more determination and passion, he now cursed decadent intellectuals and defended the right of socialist power to deal mercilessly with the 'intelligentsia' that the authorities themselves or its faithful prophets finger as enemies of the people. Who feels unfree in the Soviet Union? he asks. And though he had not spent a minute there, he replies like an insider: 'The pitiful ruins of leeches, sponges and parasites. The devil take them! We now have proof that things work a thousand times better without them. Theoretical nit-pickers, revolutionary romantics, those who, in their vanity and hatred, fail to recognize achievement. The devil take them! Decadent poets and artists. The devil take them! . . . Ten such "intellectuals" are not worth the life of a single honest worker, who could die from their acts of sabotage . . . '

Can there be more vivid proof of the depths to which the prophets were led by the blindness of their secular faith? Of how literature, which still claimed to serve the noblest interests of man, justice and a better social order, can become transformed in defence of planned enslavement and murder?

Prophets have always tended to take sides in disputes. Those who saw themselves as messengers of the divine word could compare their visions, their sense of God and His will, with those of others. Prophets of the secular faith were faced with the reality of entirely worldly experiences. The more these experiences departed from ideal notions and recent promises, the more the prophets had to paper them over, twist and embellish them. Once they had passionately, though somewhat blindly, presented life as a striving towards hope, regardless of how far off or illusory; now they were describing illusions and then presenting them as a life full of hope.

With this approach to their work and their mission, art necessarily comes to a halt. The artist becomes a mere executive, a popularizer of directives and resolutions. It is inappropriate for him to question the essence or the correctness of those resolutions. Works of the true faith were written on that basis even after the Second World War. They were no longer inspired by the original vision, merely by a utilitarian, dogmatic and power-oriented version of it. A picture on a poster has little to do with the life it refers to or with the artistic style employed, because the powers that be have commissioned it. Such a poster will hardly speak to anyone, let alone inspire them or persuade them.

Even in countries where political power commands, or at least encourages, such doctrinaire work, such creations gradually disappear. Artists begin demanding their basic right to write about life as they see it, to create in harmony with their own thinking and feeling, even if it means being persecuted, banned or jailed. It is in these countries that we would have the hardest time finding any true prophets of secular faith. The old prophets have died and left no heirs.

Socialist literature, as the most typical expression of literature inspired by doctrine (at first breathing meaning into life, but soon standing between the creator and life) thus belongs to the past. Nevertheless, like every intellectual (or pseudo-intellectual) trend, it has left behind traces of itself, or at least empty spaces, in the general way of thinking.

The constant repetition of the claim that history moves towards a specific secular goal (a higher social order, greater abundance, a better organization of human affairs) and that therefore people have the right or even the duty to use any possible means to reach that goal, has left its mark on the general cast of mind. To this day, there is a vague, but practically unshakeable conviction in the popular mind that history really does move towards a higher, secular goal. It may have been wrongly defined, improperly realized, incorrectly named, but it is still there. Not to recognize it, not to work towards it, is to deny progress (which, after all, exists; doesn't the rapid development of science and technology prove this?) As long as this conviction remains, the danger remains that some new utopian vision, some new ideology, will arise, full of bloated promises, to lead humanity towards the new goal, regardless of cost.

Many of these dogmas, predictions, laws and prophecies of socialism did not long survive the encounter with reality. But the 'language' that shaped the faith and entered general awareness through the works of those prophets proved to have much greater immunity. This 'language that is not just dead, but is the language of death itself' (Jiří Gruša) above all created a special vocabulary of taboo words or magic conjunctions whose only purpose was to correct or simplify reality so that it could then be interpreted in the spirit of the secular faith.

Think of the shifts that have taken place, in this century alone, in the general understanding of concepts like 'individualism' or 'collectivism'. Think of the stigma attached to the mere notion of 'bourgeois', 'petty bourgeois', 'conservative' or 'rightwinger', or what an aura of sanctity has surrounded notions like 'progress', 'the left', 'the people'. (Who would dare oppose the interests of the people, or at least say out loud the simple fact that most of the great crimes of our century were committed in the name of that vaguest of all concepts?) And what about the word 'revolutionary' or even 'revolution'? Nadezhda Mandelstam recalls its magic impact:

> The decisive role in winning over the intelligentsia was not played by terror and bribery (God knows there was enough of both!) but the word 'revolution' itself, which no one wanted to reject. Entire nations have succumbed to this word. It was so powerful that one wonders what our rulers still needed prisons and executions for?

Words replaced proof. Often words were enough to present as an established fact what was only the desire or the opinion of prophets. The Czech philosopher Belohradsky has called this 'the language of disrupted experience': he points out that anyone who tried to submit the language to empirical control would be accused of subjectivism or of other vices ('reactionary', naturally). If language is to regain its meaning, however, words have to be disenchanted, divested of their servitude to the secular faith and its idols, purged of the emotional ballast that outweighs their real meaning in the minds of both those who use them and those who hear them.

The history of socialist literature and the fate of its writers must often feel, to anyone who thinks about it, like a tragic history. Many of the authors wrote what they wrote and believed what they believed because they longed for a better, more just society. Their faith blinded them and that had tragic consequences for their work, for the ideas they were trying to defend, and often for themselves. When they saw the error of their ways, some tried to come to terms with this in their own work; others brought their lives to an untimely end.

Nevertheless, because we demand truthfulness and honesty in a writer, we will see what happened to them as a moral failure, not a tragedy. Their fate suggests that secular faith drains a writer of his particular qualities and ultimately of his personality. It blinds him, and distances him from reality. Secular prophets did not realize that God cannot be replaced by any profane idol, just as the best-organized social system in the world cannot buy you immortality. No matter how well intentioned, their visions must necessarily have plunged into a void, pulling their creators along with them. From the depths of that void they were no longer able to perceive the true outlines of the world and events in it; they were no longer able to reach the people they had originally wanted to address.

The writer who accepts an alien view of the world (especially one associated with power), who allows his language to be taken away from him, denies the precondition of all creation: the truthfulness he alone, in his conscience, can guarantee. It also calls into doubt the basic assumption of creation, which lies, after all, in the writer's attempt to enrich the sum total of human awareness and knowledge, of human experience, by adding to it his own search and his own discoveries. It is hard to imagine an idea so grand that it could excuse this greatest treason a writer can commit, against himself, his work and his audience.

Written for the conference organized by the Wheatland
Foundation, May 1988, Lisbon

OUR TRADITION AND THE LIMITS
OF GROWTH

WHEN THE WAR ended and I returned from the camp where I had spent almost four years of my childhood, I not only felt bitterness towards everything German, but I was also obsessed by the German theme. I devoured literature in which the authors described their suffering in the concentration camps and the cruelty of their jailers. I followed all the big war-crimes trials, as well as all the attempts to explain how it could all have happened, how a nation that had recently contributed so much to culture could have experienced so abrupt a descent into barbarity.

In later years, I met Germans who were quite different from those I had known during the war. Many of them tried hard to help me in the difficulties I was experiencing, difficulties caused by the descent of my own country into an entirely different kind of barbarity.

These circumstances, and my experiences, convinced me that this barbarization, which the writer Karel Čapek called 'one of the greatest cultural débâcles in the history of humanity', could not be blamed on a single nation or state, or on any definable human group. After all, similar declines have happened before, and I'm afraid they can happen again at any time, anywhere on our planet.

This discovery did little to ease my mind: I wanted to understand what had happened. Why, in a century in which human genius had achieved so much, had there been two devastating wars, mass exterminations and death camps? Why did people destroy in such a frenzy the things of cultural value they had so recently admired? What led so many educated people to accept without protest, or even with enthusiasm, behaviour that flew in the face of the humanistic traditions of European culture?

Available information and eyewitness accounts have established, with increasing certainty, that events in the first half of our century in Russia, Mexico, Italy, Germany, Spain and, somewhat later, in Chile or in Cambodia—while they may have had different starting-points—were remarkably similar in their cultural consequences. Did there exist a common cause that triggered, irrespective of circumstances, this sudden and stubborn veering away from the general trend of culture? Was there—in the words of Karel Čapek again—an 'immense betrayal by the intellectuals' leading to 'the barbarization of everyone'?

Of course there were reasons for this collapse that were rooted in the social and economic spheres, not just in culture, but it is the almost incomprehensible betrayal by the intellectuals that is remarkable. Did it really represent a veering away from traditional culture, from the traditions of our learning, or was it, paradoxically, an outcome of that learning?

In the introduction to his history of philosophy, Hegel wrote: 'What every generation accomplished in science, in intellectual production, is a heritage that whole generations have accumulated; it is a sacrament to which all generations of mankind gratefully and joyfully added everything that had helped them in life, everything they had mined from the depths of nature and the human spirit. To inherit in this sense means to accept it and, at the same time, to commit oneself to it.' To commit oneself to this inheritance, he explains, means to preserve and enrich everything man has been handed down from earlier ages in the field of knowledge. 'Such too is the mission and the activity of our age, and indeed of all ages: to grasp the science that exists, and to make it one's own, and in this way to develop it and raise it to a higher level.'

What Hegel says here about science can be applied to all cultural enterprise. Stress on continuity and development, and raising culture to a higher level, is an expression of a dynamism, of a capacity to accelerate that no other major culture familiar to us has ever managed to achieve to this extent. From this dynamism, other European discoveries and inventions can be seen to flow: the importance of increasingly free individuals, faith in action, in what the individual can contribute to common improvement, support for the competitiveness that stimulates such efforts.

This dynamism and the sense of responsibility for the spiritual and intellectual heritage of our predecessors are the product of centuries. Europe became civilized only gradually. Three centuries ago women were still burned at the stake for witchcraft and consorting with the devil, just as heretics were burned for holding a different set of beliefs. Nevertheless, the atmosphere in Europe began to change at the end of the eighteenth century, and cruel, age-old customs apparently died out. The nineteenth century, with its rapid development in all fields of human endeavour and in human and civic rights, confirmed our belief that the humanist tradition had finally triumphed. Even war was henceforth to be fought 'humanely': the first of a number of Geneva Conventions was concluded in 1864. Even if widespread poverty persisted and social inequality produced tensions, it seemed unimaginable that an absolutist or tyrannical government of the kind known in the past could re-establish itself anywhere in Europe, or that someone might establish a claim to control the intellectual life of a society as the church had done until recently. This age brought to perfection the notion that there were no limits to human possibilities, and gave birth to many illusions, unfounded hopes and utopian visions.

And then, during the first third of this century, those revolutionary events—and collapses—took place. If anyone gave any thought at all to a connection between this modern decline into barbarism and the traditions of European culture, the assumption was that this tradition had been raped, broken or, at least, badly misunderstood. Yet isn't the exact opposite true? Cannot the blame for these collapses be found precisely in those qualities that are the most intrinsic, the most stimulating, the most valuable: in Europe's dynamism, its competitive spirit, its progressiveness, the principle that it is man's responsibility to grasp what is here, to develop it and take it to a higher level?

Everything in us rebels against accepting such a conclusion. After all, the disastrous experiences we have had this century warn us that anyone who abandons tradition to build a new society, a new empire, a better order, opens the door to a vacuum in which the collapse takes place.

Though it is certainly imprudent to abandon tradition, we must constantly investigate and correct wrong assumptions. The idea of unending progress and improvement assumed that our opportunities, our sources, our aims should not and must not be restricted. This assumption concerned both the spiritual and the material spheres. While we now admit that it was a mistake in the material sphere, we still believe that spiritually and intellectually we can rise as high as we want without obstruction. But is this actually the case?

In 1898, the Mexican writer Victoriano Salado Alvarez wrote this remarkably far-sighted description of European civilization and culture: 'In Europe, the advantages of urban and private comfort, a variety of cheap entertainment, the clash and contradictions in theory, the extraordinary number of books, railways, telegraph lines, the distaste for everything that has already been used and the longing to try something quite new—has brought with it a certain satedness, a degeneration, a neurosis, countless forms of hysteria and many kinds of folly, among them musical and literary folly.'

If we think about modern painting, music, literature, philosophy, law or any of the other humanities (including medicine, which can now prolong the suffering or the unconsciousness of the dying for months, if not for years), we must ask ourselves whether these disciplines have come to the limits of their potential. Have they not been taken as far as they can go? Abstract painting reached the point where the artist covered the canvas with an even layer of the same colour, a single line or nothing at all. After such an act, no matter how much it may have been celebrated for its originality and innovation, there is nothing left to do. We can only see in such an act a harbinger of the end of visual art. Writers, in their search for new stories, sought inspiration in dreams, in the big-city underworld, or in the company of deranged murderers. Others tried to break up the traditional narrative, to disrupt or suspend real time. But the moment the most extreme works of Joyce or Beckett carried originality to the very limits of incomprehensibility, the literary quest had gone about as far as it could go. Beyond it a chasm opened up. The same thing has happened to philosophers. In their investigations and their language, they too moved away from problems that still interested, or were still comprehensible to, anyone who was not himself a philosopher. Were there any laymen interested in philosophy who could understand the meditations of Husserl or Carnap?

In all areas of creativity and research, enormous effort was needed to push even slightly beyond the frontiers established by one's predecessors. At the same time, in order to continue and develop, it was necessary to erode or obscure what had already been achieved, or merely give new names to old discoveries. Even to genuine spirits, the limits towered above like a wall. What lay beyond?

At the end of all effort, to paraphrase Heidegger, you can find either God, or a void.

Both education and environment have led the intellectual to see his role as developing and enriching the heritage of his precursors. If he saw no way of doing this, however, he inevitably succumbed to feelings of frustration and disappointment. How was he to resolve the conflict between what he expected of himself (and what others expected of him) and what he was, in fact, able to accomplish?

He could put enormous effort into merely overcoming the limits or he could give up. He could also try to escape: into an idealized past or an idealized future, from an area where reason was king to a place where faith (which knows no limits) reigned.

Under the impression that he was continuing in the European intellectual and spiritual tradition, the intellectual invented populist visions of salvation that were intended to put meaning back into creative work. 'It will be a free literature,' Lenin promised at the beginning of the century, when referring to a new proletarian literature, 'because it will serve not overstuffed heroines, nor a bored and obese "top 10,000", but the millions and tens of millions of workers who are the flower of the country, its strength and its future. It will be a free literature, the fertile last word of the revolutionary idea of human experience and the living work of the socialist proletariat . . . ' (Lenin: *Party Organization and Party Literature*, 1905.)

Great ideologies were fascinating either because they imagined a less problematic past or because they envisioned a harmonious future where everyone would receive everything according to his needs. Their often fantastic or naïve arguments and promises required more faith than reason, and they could scarcely have gained the massive currency they did, had the intellectuals not been dominated by feelings of disappointment, uselessness and the need to escape.

It was not just the intellectuals, however, or the creators who were disappointed, it was also the receivers, the audience. Albert Speer, who was certainly qualified to talk about the intellectual roots of Nazism, recalled something his teacher Tessenow had told to them: 'Someone who thinks in a very simple way must appear. Today's thinking has become too complicated. The uneducated person, the peasant, as he is, would deal with all these problems in a much simpler fashion because he is not yet spoiled. He also has the strength to carry out his simple ideas.' (Albert Speer, *Inside the Third Reich*, Collier, 1981, p15.) Indeed. The lives of many on the receiving end of culture had been forced into a down-to-earth simplicity that went against the spirit of the times, that acknowledged movement and change, and this disjunction must have made them uneasy. They were awaiting a meaningful, understandable message from those who spoke to them, but instead they only received more, often provocative examples of the innovative spirit. Audiences felt that the intellectuals had left them behind. This could have caused bitterness or, equally, an indifference to intellectual and spiritual values, but the chief effect was to open many souls to pseudo-values, simplified visions of an idealized past or a redemptive future.

Audiences parted company with the intellectuals who had so far remained faithful to what they understood as their calling, to develop the values that they had inherited, and joined up with those who, like them, were looking for an escape. They met in a common downfall that was all the more headlong because there was no one to apply the brakes.

In this connection, it is worth considering why totalitarian systems, whatever ideology they espoused, rejected modern art and the modern humanitarian sciences as incomprehensible, degenerate or alien. The usual explanation is that they were afraid of innovation, afraid of unconventional thinking and expression. In reality they had merely guessed, correctly, that they would win favour with the majority, that more would share their condemnation of modern thinking and art than would be upset, even among disappointed intellectuals. I would not dare to claim this had I not, in my own youth, experienced the remarkable conversion of avant-garde artists, who had once sworn by experimentation, into apostles of a primitive socialist realism. They now swore by a literature that was understandable to 'millions of working people'. Many, of course, did so out of self-interest or fear, but also because they believed that this was a way to escape the bind they were in and come closer to their audiences. (The fact that the totalitarian system quickly lost favour with intellectuals, as well as with this 'audience', is another matter. The very essence of these systems, their crude recourse to force, soon alienated them from all creative people.)

These events were so complex that they cannot be explained by a single cause, nor was that my intention. I merely wanted to point out the reality of limits in the intellectual sphere. All intellectual effort, both now and in the future, will have to come to terms with them. The problem will be more urgent than ever.

Those who draw attention to limits of growth in the material sphere and demand that we alter our expectations, our goals or our way of life, are not asking us to return to the Stone Age. If we admit to limits in the intellectual sphere, it does not mean we are asking for a return to barbarism, or that we are rejecting tradition, even if it was sometimes based on false assumptions. Quite the contrary. The dynamism of our culture, after all, assumes a capacity for constant self-evaluation, for an awareness of every threat to itself. That means it should also be able to curtail its own impetuosity and its own megalomania should these prove dangerous.

Once again I return to Karel Čapek, who half a century ago, overwhelmed by the collective collapse of the intellectuals, and intellectuality, tried to define the mission of culture in our time: 'To know something, at least, about experiences, the knowledge and values humanity has already created—and not to lose ground, not to slip beneath that level. Yes, let's say it outright: education is, in this sense, conservation . . . Culture represents, first of all, the coherence of all human activity so far; it must not lose that . . . To defend that is just as serious a struggle as to take new positions by storm and conquer them. The human spirit would be a bad soldier if it only felt qualified to march in the vanguard . . . without being able to defend what it had already conquered.'

No one is assuming that, in this day and age, a place can no longer be found for creative spirits who lift the veil from some previously unrevealed mystery, or make whole something that appeared imperceptibly in decline. But we ought to be drawing conclusions from the cultural collapses the century has brought with it. An age that rated so highly virtues such as rapid development, competitiveness, change, progress, innovation and modernity, often at the expense of other values, is over. It carried creative people in many fields to within reach of the limits of the possible, the acceptable, the usable or at least the comprehensible. The work of many of the top contemporary thinkers and artists indicates that they are aware of this. For example, my compatriot Milan Kundera evolved a remarkable form in his novels that went back to the roots of our literary tradition, to a period when philosophical or historical reflection were as much a part of literature as narrative or prophetic vision. Regardless of their complexity or originality, Kundera's novels speak to a contemporary audience. His work is symptomatic of the times we are moving into, which ought to be more 'ecological'. It ought to defend and preserve former values, to try to make them generally known and thus shared. It would not scorn intellectuals who are 'merely' seeking a language we could all understand and thus attempting to reduce the dangerous distances between those who work in different branches of the arts and sciences. For increasingly we are all appearing in both roles: insiders who are high up in their field, and outsiders, passive audiences, who are down there with everyone else.

Delivered at a session of the Swedish National Committee for Cultural Cooperation in Europe, Stockholm, October 1990

V

THE SWORDS ARE APPROACHING: FRANZ KAFKA'S SOURCES OF INSPIRATION

UNTIL I WAS twenty-five, I knew nothing of Franz Kafka. By this time—the early fifties—I had graduated in Czech literature and linguistics at Prague University, but our lecturers had never mentioned this native of Prague. And it was inconceivable, at the time, that he should be included in a history of Czech literature.

In 1957, an anthology of ten novellas by important twentieth-century authors was published in Prague. The final item was Kafka's 'In the Penal Colony'. Until then, my studies had consisted entirely of realistic prose, yet despite this—or perhaps because of it—Kafka's story had a powerful impact on me. Its message, I had no doubt, concerned my own life. Had I not, only a few years before, been like the innocent prisoner forced to lie on the 'bed' of an execution machine? I had witnessed uniformed executioners who felt that their monstrous activity was equally logical and infallible—who also presented it as an act of justice. I, too, felt I had been miraculously saved, called back from the gas chamber, just as the condemned soldier was called back from the brink.

Like almost everyone who had spent time in a concentration camp, I read books filled with horrifying details of those murderous institutions, so many that my mind began to resist them. Yet Kafka's image of a desert valley with its engine of torture and its fantastic operator engraved itself on my memory. I cannot recall reading any work of literature that has affected me so deeply.

I

SEEN FROM THE outside, the life of Franz Kafka unfolded in an orderly, almost monotonous fashion. A well-behaved young man who finished high school with some reluctance and studied law in a desultory fashion. A model office clerk who dispassionately carried out his duties in an insurance company, gradually, even reluctantly, working his way up through the ranks. A confirmed bachelor, who tried in vain to overcome a deep aversion to marriage. Broken engagements, holidays spent mostly in Austrian or Bohemian spas. Nocturnal writing. Physical indispositions: insomnia, migraines, hypochondria. At the end of his life, a terminal lung condition. Several friendships, several interests that, given the nature of his work, may appear surprisingly mundane—agriculture, gardening, swimming—not unlike the interests of the average citizen. He was not religious and took only a passive interest in politics, even though the Prague police once detained him at an anarchist meeting of sorts. He was a Jew, he lived in the Czech world of Prague and he wrote in German, but these contradictions do not seem to have interfered with his daily life.

If Kafka's personal life tended to be uneventful, the same cannot be said of the times in which he lived. He wrote most of his work during one of the most turbulent periods in history. When he was thirty-one, a world war broke out, and though he did not have to enlist, he could not escape its consequences. The level of hunger and misery in Prague was difficult to imagine. Mutilation, pain and violent death were all around him. Then came a peace that changed the face of Europe. Prague— Kafka's birthplace—became the capital of the new Czechoslovak republic. Then came revolutions in Hungary and Germany, and social unrest elsewhere, even in Prague. There was civil war in Russia.

Writers were, for the most part, swept up in events, in external activity. They believed they had to bear witness, to warn, to show the way out of the catastrophe, to seek a better way of organizing society. Their works were consumed by revolutionary events and ideas.

There is almost none of this in Kafka's work. On 2 August 1914, there are only two sentences in his diary: 'Germany has declared war on Russia.—Swimming in the afternoon.' [1] This linking of an insignificant personal detail with a matter of world-shattering importance, could, or ought to, stand as a motto, a key to every consideration of Kafka's work. The external world of the time was different from the world in which he moved. In his diaries or his correspondence, it is astonishing how completely he focused his attention on himself, his feelings, his pain, his inadequacies, his illnesses, his dreams, his anxieties, his most trivial, everyday activities. 'He did not have the same lightness of touch for his private and inner life that distinguishes minor writers from writers with imagination,' was how Elias Canetti put it. [2] And Kafka himself, at the beginning of the war, notes: 'Immediate contact with the everyday world robs me of a broad view of things, as though I were standing at the bottom of a ravine, and with my head down.' [3]

To understand the meaning and circumstances of Kafka's work, one must first seek the laws and the order of his inner world.

The Prague law student lived an apparently quiet life. He never suffered hunger as Charles Dickens did, nor was he ever taken out to be executed as Dostoevsky had been, nor did he experience the horrors of marching off to war like so many of his contemporaries. Yet this does not mean his inner life was not dramatic, that it was not governed by passion, or that imaginary firing squads never pointed their guns at him.

In one of his letters to the Czech journalist, translator and writer Milena Jesenská, Kafka said of himself: 'I am mentally ill; the illness in my lungs is merely a mental illness that has moved inland. I've been ill in this way for four or five years, ever since my first engagement to marry.' [4] Though Kafka tended to exaggerate his weaknesses, incapacities and indispositions, there is no doubt that his spirit was as vulnerable as his body. At the end of his life, he still remembered the inner wounds inflicted by his father, who would punish him by waking him at night and locking him on the balcony, alone. He felt wounded where others, later in life, might have seen it as nothing more than standard parental discipline. His father taught him mistrust, the causes of which remained hidden. 'The mistrust towards most people that, in the shop and at home, you tried to inculcate in me . . . and which, oddly, did not particularly encumber you . . . this mistrust, which was not confirmed in my own eyes as a young boy—for everywhere I saw only people who were admirable beyond reach—was transformed in me into mistrust of myself, and into constant fear of everything else.' [5]

'For him, life is something utterly different from what it is for everyone else. Money, the stock exchange, the foreign exchange market, typewriters—he sees them as mystical things . . . For him they are strange puzzles—his relationship to them is completely different from ours.' This is how Milena Jesenská characterized him. 'Do you think his office job is just ordinary work? For him an office—even his own—is something as mysterious and remarkable as a locomotive is to a small child. He doesn't understand the simplest things in this world.' [6]

A world that cannot be stripped of its mystery, that can be neither accommodated nor understood, becomes a labyrinth, entry to which can be gained through many portals, all of them locked and guarded. It is a world that evokes anxiety and uncertainty. 'What good fortune it is to understand that the earth upon which you stand can be no bigger than the area covered by your feet.' [7]

'He feels imprisoned in this world; he feels confined; sadness and inertia overwhelm him; sick with the mad fantasies of prisoners, he is beyond consolation precisely because that is all it is, a fragile, headache-inducing consolation that stands against the crude fact of imprisonment.' [8] The world is a mountain so steep it cannot be climbed. 'If you were walking on level ground and trying hard to move forward but making no progress, it would be a source of despair, but because you are scrambling up a steep slope, as steep as you yourself appear when seen from below, that feeling of impotence may also be merely the result of an inclination in the terrain, and you have no reason to despair.' [9] The world would always seem to be threatening to undo Kafka, and he would always flee, would always 'bolt the windows and the doors against the world,' [10] and

then again determine to do battle with it. 'No one can be satisfied with mere knowledge, he must also try to act according to
what he knows. Yet he was not given the strength for that, and
therefore he must destroy himself, though there is a danger that
he will not be granted the necessary strength even for that, yet
there is nothing else to be done but this extreme experiment.' [11]

In that struggle, Kafka never found the necessary strength,
and he would always draw back from the summit. He would see
it as a humiliating defeat, as proof of his inability to grow up and
become independent, to step beyond the frontiers of immaturity,
where he at least felt protected. 'I will never reach the age of
manhood,' he lamented. 'I shall change from a child directly into
a white-haired old man.' [12] At the age of twenty-nine, he noted:
'Given my contemptibly childish appearance, I also thought
myself unworthy to fashion a serious, responsible notion of a
great and manly future for myself. That usually seemed so
impossible to me that every little step forward seemed false, and
the next step unattainable.' [13]

Towards the end of his life, Kafka's behaviour became styl-
ized and somehow boyish. He always tried to overwhelm the
women he was interested in with accounts of his suffering, his
fear, his weaknesses, his loneliness, his illnesses. He tried to
gain their sympathy. In an almost touching diary entry early in
1912, he explains why, for lack of strength, he had to give up
all his interests and joys for the sake of his writing. 'My development is now over. As far as I can judge, I have sacrificed everything that could be sacrificed, and there is now nothing left but
to divest myself of my office job . . . so that I can begin to live a
genuine life, in which, along with the progress of my work, my
face will finally be capable of natural ageing.' [14]

It is known, however, that Kafka never voluntarily left his
job, just as he never had a family, nor ever completed one of
his longer works.

For Kafka, intense introspection took the place of his
inability to alter the circumstances of his life. If he remained
passive—and seemed helpless—the moment he turned his back
on life he became its master. Through brilliant deduction he
foresaw all the variables of his situation and prepared himself
for all his future—and certainly more successful—engagements

with life. The ambiguity and the contradictions of the world, the complexity of things, everything his spirit refused to accept, could be analysed and described, and thus rendered, if not entirely harmless, then at least bearable. Even his own 'self' could be divided into a creature with which one agrees, one side of which is recognizable, even attractive, and another which one fears or loathes.

Again and again, however, life proved more complicated than even the cleverest mind could grasp. A hundred times he prepared for marriage to Felice Bauer or for a rendezvous with Milena Jesenská, listing his arguments for and against, preparing every step in advance, and still things fell apart the moment they began to happen, thus exposing even more the painful absence of action. 'He has a double vision: the first is tranquil, full of life, lacking the certain comfort of impossible reflection, consideration, examination, gushing forth. Their number and possibilities are endless, for even nettles, if they are to take root, require a relatively large crack in the wall. But these activities require no place at all. Even where there isn't the slightest crack, thousands and thousands of them can live mutually entwined. That is the first vision. The second, however, is a moment when one is summoned to present accounts and cannot utter a syllable, and is thrown back on reflection. But now, not having the slightest prospects, he can no longer just flounder around, grow heavy and drown with a curse.' [15]

'The confinement of introspection, if it is not ventilated by an act,' said Kierkegaard, one of Kafka's favourite writers, 'produces only contemptible rancour.' [16] Kafka, incapable of rancour towards anyone around him, turned it against himself. He was bitter about his looks, his body ('I, a forest animal, was at the time scarcely in the woods. I lay somewhere in a filthy pit—filthy only as a consequence of my own presence, of course.' [17]) He hated his weaknesses, his job, his bachelorhood, his own existence, which he felt was a source of guilt. He demeaned everything he was most concerned about: his spirit, his abilities, his talent, his work. He damaged his body, and thought about destroying everything he wrote.

Life that is not enriched by action, and strives instead for introspection, becomes increasingly less comprehensible, less definable, more hostile. It arouses anxiety and exhaustion.

His diary, his letters to Felice and Milena, are full of this weariness and anxiety. It is the anxiety of the small, unwitting child in a big world, of the knowing person afraid to think things through, to achieve, to transform what he understands into action. 'You are thirty years old and you are wearier than old age could make you. Or, more precisely, you are not weary at all, merely restless, and you are afraid of taking a single step in this world, which is one huge trap. That's why you will always have both feet in the air.' [18] 'It is certain that away from you, I cannot live unless I acknowledge my fears, and I do it without compulsion, with pleasure, I pour myself into it . . . It's an odd thing about fear: I don't know its inner laws, I know only its hand on my throat, and that it is truly the most awful thing I have ever experienced.' [19]

Everything pulls Kafka away from this world, to a place where things and human relationships maintain their mystery, where it is he who decides on the shape of things, where he can be both the condemned and the judge, both the hunted and the hunter, the king and the messenger, where he can be happy for at least a little while, as long as he is able to 'hold the world up in purity, truth and immutability'. [20]

II

IT IS INTERESTING that an artist who has had so many books and articles written about him, who seduced many lesser writers to imitation and who considered literature, or at least his own writing, as the most important thing in his life, wrote so little about literature and his literary convictions.

Unless goaded into it, or asked a direct question, Kafka was not in the habit, even in his letters, of talking about anything that did not immediately concern himself. Ideas, philosophical systems, books by others—everything remained beyond the sphere of his immediate interest, as did the campaigns in the war, speeches by politicians or foreign revolutions. Kafka was not at all an intellectual author. He had no illusions about his capacity to think theoretically: 'I have no memory for things I have learned, nor things I have read, nor things experienced or heard, neither for people nor events; I feel that I have experienced nothing, learned nothing, that I actually know less than the average schoolboy, and that what I do know is superficial, and that every second question is beyond me. I am incapable of thinking deliberately; my thoughts run into a wall. I can grasp the essence of things in isolation, but I am quite incapable of coherent, unbroken thinking. I can't even tell a story properly; in fact, I can scarcely talk . . . '[21] Oddly, he put this self-evaluation in a letter asking Felice Bauer to marry him. Some time later, he recorded in his diary: 'The difficulties . . . I have when speaking to people comes from the fact that my thinking, or rather the contents of my consciousness, are foggy. That doesn't bother me as far as I myself am concerned; I'm sometimes even satisfied with myself. But conversing with people requires the ability to give what one says a point, to maintain the unity and the coherence of the conversation, and these are not qualities I possess. No one wants to lie about with me in clouds of fog, and even if they did, they could not drive the fog from my head.' [22]

These assessments of his own thinking, regardless of how exaggerated they are, may—like all of Kafka's negative self-evaluations—be understood as a symptom of his distaste for complex theoretical thinking. Even if Kafka had enjoyed logical analysis and liked mulling over the possibilities inherent in situations that life offered, his inspiration lay, for the most part, in the primary world of his own experiences, one might even say his basic, existential experiences, and not in the mediated sphere of ideas. It is true that these experiences took on an almost dreamlike visual form, and from those images—consciously or unconsciously—he composed a new reality, a new world often so far removed from its original inspiration that it lost the clarity and force of the immediate experience. Many apparently illogical connections, relationships and symbols have seduced readers into seeking widely varied and often contradictory interpretations—intellectual codes in Kafka's works that could be deciphered and traced back to an original idea, either religious or philosophical. But this approach is based on a basic misconception about how Kafka worked, and it has interfered with our acceptance and understanding of his work.

'In the Penal Colony' is one of the longest of Kafka's completed works. Compared with his other writing, the setting is exotic, and the description of the torture machine and how it works reveals the author's sadism. It is unusual, also, in that Kafka, who usually identifies with his heroes, appears in this story to vacillate between the two protagonists. 'The difficulty that Kafka's writing, and "In the Penal Colony" in particular, offer the reader stems from the fact that Kafka himself has taken a stand somewhere between the officer and the Explorer.' [23]

There are several relationships in the story that are difficult to 'decipher', the most important and complex of which appears to be the relationship of the officer to his machine. What exactly is this horrific machine supposed to symbolize? And what of the orders that have to be inserted into it? Why can't the explorer read them? Why does the machine break down at precisely the moment the officer lies down on its 'bed'? What is the meaning of the handkerchief that changes hands, from the condemned man to the officer and then back again? Why does the officer choose death? Only because the explorer refused to support him? Why is the grave of the old commander found, absurdly, inside a tearoom? What does the inscription on his grave mean?

Many contradictory interpretations have been offered for this story. It can be understood as the depiction of a cruel law, or it can represent the dehumanization of a warring society. The story's imagery apparently demonstrates how our machine civilization has merged with a barbarian tradition and shows the monstrous outcome of this union. Symbolically, it represents the act of writing as bloody self-sacrifice. Or, it presents a cruel, archaic religious tradition: the torture machine can be decoded 'as an altar, where man is sacrificed in the name of a monstrous idol—the law'. The destruction of the machine 'becomes the basis for the advent of a new age, one that is more humane, more rational.' [24]

What is striking about this story is not the exotic locale (which in any case is as nondescript as it is in most of Kafka's prose works) but the fantastic and detailed description of the execution machine. Technical description of any kind is rare in Kafka's work. ('The Aeroplanes of Brescia' is only a journalistic sketch, which Kafka wrote at Max Brod's suggestion. [25]) If a telephone switchboard, or a table with a regulator appears as it does in *America*, or a measuring device in 'Visit to the Mine', the technology is only incidental. But now, suddenly, a third of the text in one of his longest works is taken up with a description of this monstrous machine and how it works. True, the author interrupts his description in several places, but he keeps coming back to it, as if to reinforce the idea that the machine is the most important thing in the story, and everything else merely incidental.

If most of Kafka's stories draw their subject matter from his innermost experiences, then what experience can the image of the torture machine represent? In one of his letters to Milena Jesenská (written after the story), he writes: 'You know, when I try to write something [about our engagement] the swords whose points surround me in a circle begin slowly to approach the body, it's the most complete torture; when they begin to graze me it's already so terrible that at the first scream I betray you, myself, everything . . .' [26]

Kafka was terrified by the prospect of marriage. The image he uses in the letter recalls precisely his picture of the torture machine—and thus it is instructive to examine Kafka's circumstances when he was writing 'In the Penal Colony'.

The first mention of this story appears in Kafka's diary in the autumn of 1914, along with references to the opening chapters of *The Trial*. Both works follow immediately upon two events that marked Kafka for life. After a two-year acquaintance with Felice Bauer, Kafka proposed to her on 1 June, in the Bauers' house in Berlin. But just six weeks later, again in Berlin, a strange meeting took place in the Hotel Askanische Hof. Besides Kafka and Felice, there were several others present, among them Felice's sister Erna and her friend Greta Bloch. In his diary, Kafka refers to this meeting as 'the trial'. Clearly Kafka's future marriage was discussed. Before witnesses, the fiancée expressed her fears and her criticisms of the future bridegroom, and above all, she 'publicized' her notions of what their life together would be like. To Kafka, this was unacceptable. He did not see marriage as an end in itself, as the fulfilment of his life, and he rejected the idea of a petit-bourgeois household. 'Not only do I not need such a home, the very idea of it terrifies me.'[27] He tried to explain his ambivalence. 'There have always been—and remain—two warring selves within me. One of them is the kind of person you would wish him to be, and if he were to develop somewhat further, he might achieve the little it would take to make your wish come true. Nothing of which you accused me in the Hotel Askanische Hof related to him in the least. The second self, however, thinks of nothing but work; that is his only interest. The two selves are locked in a struggle, but it is not an ordinary struggle in which they merely go at each other with their fists. The first self is dependent on the second; he will never . . . triumph. On the contrary, he is pleased when the second self is victorious, and when it appears that the second is losing, the first immediately kneels before him and takes no account of anything but him.'[28] Of course Kafka told his fiancée all this three months later. During the 'trial' itself, he remained silent. The group Felice brought with her took him by surprise. He remained silent, however, not in defiance, but because he had no essential objections to what she said. 'I understood that everything was lost . . . I could have saved the situation only by making some marvellous confession, but there was none I could possibly have made.'[29]

Six weeks later the engagement was broken off. Kafka visited Felice's parents one more time and then wrote to her. He described it as a 'letter written under the gallows'.[30] Immediately afterwards, he went to the seaside for two weeks with his friend Ernst Weiss (who had opposed the engagement to Felice). Kafka described the engagement briefly in his diary: 'He was bound hand and foot like a criminal. If they had put me in a corner, in real chains, and put policemen in front of me and left me there to watch, it could not have been worse. And it was my engagement; they all tried to bring me to life and when they did not succeed, to take me as I was. F. the least of any of them, quite justly, of course, because she was suffering the most. What for the rest was a transitory event was a threat to her.'[31]

This is not unlike the initial image in 'In the Penal Colony', where, 'besides the officer and the traveller there was only the condemned man, a dull-looking man with a wide mouth, shabby hair and a dissolute face, and the soldier holding the heavy chain, to which ran smaller chains fastened around the prisoner's ankles and wrists . . . The prisoner, in any case, had such a look of doglike submissiveness about him that it seemed as if they could let him run free about the hillsides—they would only have to whistle and he would come running . . . ' [32]

The obsessive detail in which the officer describes his machine suggests that he is preoccupied with it to the exclusion of all else, yet he is not merely the prisoner's executioner, he is also the prosecuting attorney and judge.

This revelation—during the first break in the description of the machine—echoes the basic situation of *The Trial*. The officer informs the explorer of the prisoner's offence, the essence of which was that when his superior officer whipped him, the prisoner cried out, 'Throw that whip away or I'll eat you!' In other words, his crime was merely that he tried to fend off physical violence with a verbal threat. It also becomes apparent that the prisoner—like Josef K. in *The Trial*—does not know the judgement handed down to him. 'It would be pointless to declare it. After all, he will experience it himself,' claims the officer. [33] Nor does the accused have any opportunity to defend himself. There is no reason for it, he is told. 'The principle according to which I always decide is this: guilt is always indubitable.' [34] The officer's statement is repeated almost word for word by the painter Titorelli in *The Trial*, when he says that, 'As soon as the court arraigns someone, it is firmly persuaded of his guilt.' [35]

Josef K. is never given the opportunity to defend himself properly. Kafka, too, remained silent during his Berlin 'tribunal'. The prisoner in the story even has a felt-covered stick shoved into his mouth. Thus the prisoner and the explorer/witness listen silently to the officer's matter-of-fact, enthusiastic and terrifying explanation. They learn that the execution takes twelve hours. For the first six hours, the prisoner will apparently live as he has before (an incredible claim, given the suffering the prisoner is subjected to, but the time period may actually relate to another reality, for the engagement dinner may have lasted twelve hours, and it took six weeks for Kafka to conclude that the state in which he found himself was fatefully dangerous to him.) 'But after about six hours, how the man will fall silent! Even the thickest person in the world will begin to see the light.' [36] For the next six hours, nothing happens; the prisoner, through his wounds, merely deciphers the contents of the verdict. Then the 'gates pierce him and throw him into a pit, where he falls into a bed of bloody water and cotton wool. The trial is over . . . ' [37]

While the tribunal in *The Trial* is corruptible, base and wretched, the officer in the penal colony is utterly devoted to his business, his truth. Even if what he describes appears as ghastly, bloody murder, the officer is convinced that he is defending a tried, true and traditional ritual enactment of the most exalted justice. As soon as he understands that everything is about to turn against him, that his efforts to maintain the cere-mony, to save the machine and thus the 'legacy of his old commander', have failed, he writes, as a condemnation of his own guilt: 'Be just!' But the explorer, to whom he gives these two words, cannot read them anyway. 'Perhaps I believe,' he says, 'that those words are written here.' [38]

When the officer has programmed the machine to kill him and then self-destruct (the machine cannot survive his death, just as a marriage cannot be concluded without the other partner), he pulls two lady's handkerchiefs from under his collar and tosses them to the prisoner. It is one of two casual, almost dreamy allusions to a female element and thus to the real in-spiration of this story.

It is now certain which character Kafka really identifies with: the prisoner, who was brought in helpless, burdened with guilt but ignorant of his crime, to be confronted by a machine that works in conformity with ancient, illegible, indecipherable orders and ancient but hostile laws. Moreover, thanks to the intervention of external powers, the cruel logic of the tribunal is miraculously and coincidentally overturned and used against the accuser. The victim escapes, though not from the Island, which only the explorer, the witness, can leave. The victim, then, does not even escape the reach of the torture machine, nor its representatives, to which the prophecy on the tombstone in the tearoom applies.

Franz Kafka managed to board the boat with his friend. He left the tribunal a free man and went to the sea, which appears so tellingly at the end of the story. But his next hero, Josef K., does not escape the executioners and endures an even stranger trial with him.

III

KAFKA BEGAN WORK on *The Trial* soon after he returned from the 'Berlin tribunal'. The experience of torture that precedes the execution is spread over twelve months (as opposed to twelve hours in 'In the Penal Colony'). It takes the form of a trial to which the accused is subjected by a mysterious and inaccessible tribunal. As in the penal colony story, the question of guilt is not the subject of examination. The accused has practically no hope of liberation. The essence, then, is this tortured experience of an unfolding trial from which there is no escape, in which even the best defence has no chance of a hearing.

The trial opens with a familiar scene: strange men burst into Josef K.'s flat when he is asleep and desecrate his privacy. The desecrators bring in more and more witnesses, widening the painful net they are drawing around him. The early scenes contain nothing about the crime, the character of the tribunal nor the laws it administers, although more and more new witnesses appear. Watchmen enter, and a supervisor awaits Josef K. The landlady appears. An old woman who lives opposite drags an old man to the window from which both of them watch everything that takes place in Josef K.'s flat. In the corner of the room where the supervisor is waiting for him, three young men unexpectedly show up. In the window across the road, a third old person appears. 'Get away from here!' Josef K. shouts at him. He feels ambushed and surrounded. 'Nosy, inconsiderate people,' he says of his onlookers. His sense of humiliation grows. In the three young men, he recognizes three colleagues from work.

The trial continues. Josef K. is told that a little investigation will be conducted into his behaviour. The investigation does not take place and never will. The investigating judge utters only a few sentences, from which it becomes apparent that he was expecting not Josef K., but a house-painter.

K. makes a speech in which he analyses the situation. The substance of this speech, or more precisely, some of its details, are no more surprising than the place he delivers it. It can be summarized in several points:

1. K. announces that he is not the person they think he is.

2. K. claims that the whole procedure will makes sense only if he himself acknowledges it. He is willing to acknowledge it only for a moment, and only from sympathy.

3. K. takes a kind of notebook from the investigating judge. It is supposed to contain material pertaining to his case, but he discovers that it is a record of debt.

4. K. declares: 'What has happened to me, of course, is merely an individual case, and it is not particularly serious because I myself do not particularly admit it, but it is a matter typical of the procedure brought against many people. It is for them that I stand here, not for myself.'

5. K. recalls the circumstances of his arrest. 'The fact of my arrest is, in itself, a laughing matter, but that is not of concern here. I was taken this morning in my bed . . . The room next door was occupied by two crude guards. If I were a dangerous robber, better precautions could not have been taken.' K. complains about the arbitrary nature of the act and the fact that it took place in front of many witnesses. The purpose of this, he says, was 'to spread the news of my arrest, and to damage my public esteem.'

6. Finally, K. reveals that behind his arrest, and the tribunal, stands an entire organization whose purpose is to arrest innocent people, to begin nonsensical procedures that are corrupt. Thus 'innocent people, instead of being heard, are to be humiliated in front of whole assemblies of people.' The people in the room react stormily to K.'s words. When he finishes, however, K. realizes that all those present, whether they respond positively or negatively to his words, are wearing a similar insignia on the collars of their coats. It is only now, when it is all over, that K. understands that he is speaking to his enemies. 'Why, you're all

clerks, as I see. You are the very corrupt band of people I've been speaking against.'

Why does K. take part in any of this when he has been mistaken for someone else? Why will the procedure only make sense if he himself acknowledges it? And with whom does he feel the sympathy that leads him to acknowledge the procedure? Why does the judge have a book of debts instead of the proper documents? After all, it may be assumed that the 'head clerk of a big bank who leads a respectable bachelor's life has no debts.' More surprising is K.'s declaration that his case is one of many, and that he understands it as representative and typical. Up to that point, it appears that K. is overwhelmed by the whole affair, that he has become the object of a mysterious, extraordinary procedure and that he knows nothing about the fact that it is 'directed against many'. And why did the court convene in a private flat? Why, instead of undergoing an interrogation, does K. deliver an indictment? Why are all those present wearing an insignia that K. doesn't notice until the very end? What is the meaning of the sensual encounter between the laundry woman and the unknown man in the middle of Josef K.'s speech?

There can be no doubt that in this scene the author is presenting an independent reality through images, for the sheer number of arbitrary or even self-contradictory facts, events and remarks is surprising. But it is precisely the arbitrariness—or apparent arbitrariness—with which Kafka puts together entirely unrelated elements that has often led to erroneous interpretations.

With his engagement in Berlin, Kafka's introspective fears about his way of life, about the possibility of continuing to write at night, surfaced. His long journey to the hotel in Berlin foreshadowed the wandering of Josef K. when he was looking for the place he was invited to for the investigation. Unlike Kafka, however, Josef K. takes the opportunity at the tribunal to present his defence. Considering that Josef K. knows neither the charges, nor the nature of the strange court, his speech can be read as a defence of Franz Kafka.

Kafka's first objection was this: I am not who you think I am. I am not a worthy husband, and I have no desire to lead the kind of life my fiancée wishes to lead. Your tribunal is therefore nonsensical, but I acknowledge it and submit to it because I sympathize with her. You wish to remind me that I am a debtor, but I have not yet become one. (The notion of marriage as a great debt emerged in Kafka's mind: 'Now the time has come to draw up a balance sheet, i.e. that attempt at marriage. And given the large investment required, the fact is that there would never have been the slightest profit from it; everything is just one huge debt . . . ' Kafka wrote in the conclusion of his 'Letter to my Father'.)

The strangeness, the dreamlike illogicality of much of Kafka's prose, which contrasts with his strictly logical deductions and coldly factual descriptions, has come about precisely as these original actions and experiences mingle with their proper imagistic form, as the world of original experiences merges with the world of parable and transforms it from an ordinary metaphor or allegory into something typically Kafkaesque. Yet this intermingling of two levels of reality is not merely a source of the special impact and urgency of Kafka's world, it is also a source of its inconsistency. That is, the point of view from which the story appears to be told, or from which a problem is seen, is also transformed. If Josef K. came into being as Kafka's double and his mysterious trial was an image of his own most personal 'trials', it was impossible to maintain this parallel throughout the entire structure of the novel. Josef K. is also a bachelor and his profession is something like that of his creator, but he lacks an entire dimension—that second self that thinks only of writing, the second self with which Franz K., clerk and husband-to-be, struggled, before whom he knelt, and for whose sake he surrendered all hope of concluding his 'trial' through mutual concession. Josef K. cannot have this second self, or at least it cannot be exposed to view, because in doing so his creator would reveal what was meant to remain secret, he would have made obvious what he most feared to lose, his own privacy. Therefore Josef K.'s situation can only be a partial parable of the real 'trials' of Franz K.

Franz K. had reason to cling to his privacy, to a way of life in which his evenings, at least, belonged exclusively to him. But why should Josef K. cling to something like that? That which for Franz K. was explicable and transparent, appears inexplicable and opaque to Josef K. Where Franz K. sensed the origins of his suffering, Josef K. encounters mystery. When Franz K. struggled to take part in the kind of life that others (and he himself) took for granted, he felt divided into two warring beings. Josef K., at the most, listens to the priest's parable of the guard and the man confronting the law, who are connected by the clash of their interests, that is, a struggle in which the latter, the one who wishes to enter the law, can never overcome the former; where Franz K. struggled for his writing, for the meaning of his life, for his freedom, Josef K. struggles only for his reputation and tries only to return to his former life—the most that could be said about which was that it was orderly and proper. Franz K. knew his tribunal and the indictment; Josef K. knows neither, and he tries again and again to make sense of both. Franz K. sensed the fateful nature of his offence, for that is what the dispute was about. Josef K. knows nothing except his humiliation, and he tries to shake that off. But just as Franz K. could not survive without bearing the stigma of his offence, or justify himself in the eyes of those who recognized another order of values, another law, Josef K. cannot survive his humiliation, his sense of shame.

That Kafka was unable to separate himself completely enough from the self in his hero explains why Josef K., in the conclusion of the novel, appears to bear something of the guilt Franz K. felt for having always 'gone into life at twentieth hand, and, moreover, for an unpraiseworthy end', as though he were endowed with the ability to see, at the very end, the light that shines from the law, a light that he himself never really sought.

The Trial, however, is not about guilt. Rather, it shows the hero as a man taken by surprise and violated; a victim, not a criminal. Josef K. does not seek out his own guilt; he looks for ways to defend himself. And because his innocence is obvious (the charges are never even stated), he looks primarily for a place where he can deliver his defence, and for those who might deliver it for him.

He is sentenced to death not because he is guilty, but because the court is prejudiced, deaf, inaccessible and unshakeable in its belief that the moment it lays charges, the accused is guilty and therefore condemned. In other words, 'a single executioner could replace this entire court.'[39]

However mysterious the court, however inaccessible its

magistrates, it conceals nothing metaphysical within it: it is a human court, even though it is endowed with a kind of omnipresence. The judges are vain, lewd, corrupt and wretched. Their power resides in their institution, in their hierarchy, in their numbers, in their hidden influence and in their unwillingness or inability to hear the words of the accused. To the very end, Josef K. is convinced of his innocence. 'How can a man be guilty at all? After all, we are all human beings, each one like the other . . . ' But he knows that everyone 'who has a part in this procedure is prejudiced against me . . . My position is therefore more difficult.' [40] Yet the moment he enters the room where the trial is to take place, he succumbs to the feeling that he has no chance of being released. The awareness that he is the subject of a trial and that everyone knows about it evokes in him a feeling of anxiety and persecution. He tries, however, to discover more about his crime and to find someone who might have influence on the outcome and who would therefore listen to his defence. But his efforts come to nothing. This fruitlessness—the fact that he knows his efforts to defend himself are pointless—at least partially explains the sudden resignation with which Josef K. accepts, and indeed awaits, his executioners.

The battle of two selves within Franz K. could never end, for neither could be changed, or made to agree, 'without being destroyed.' [41] Whereas Josef K. looks for a way out of a trial that seems to him absurd, Franz K. knew that escape is futile, that death would, in a sense, bring him relief, an end to the struggle that exhausted his powers. Franz K. was willing to walk into the abandoned quarry and die there, but because Josef K. is inseparably bound to him not only in his struggle, but in his awareness that one cannot live without the other, Josef K. dies in the quarry having learned nothing about his crime; he dies only with a feeling of humiliation. 'It is as though the shame had to survive him.'

IV

KAFKA'S WHOLE LIFE seemed to oscillate between two anxieties: fear of loneliness and fear of intimacy, which could deprive him of his world, his capacity to write. Time and again he longed to escape from the loneliness 'that can only end in punishment.'[42] He even made a third effort to become engaged, this time to Julia Wohryzkova, but what attracted him to her was probably nothing more than his desperate attempt to put an end to his loneliness.

At the age of almost thirty-eight, he made one more passionate and desperate attempt to escape his isolation by living with a woman he loved and thus fulfil his life by marrying.

He began his final great emotional relationship in the usual way: letters went back and forth almost daily between Merano and Vienna, between Franz Kafka and Milena Jesenská. But this superficial resemblance to his earlier relationship is as far as it goes. Milena was the first woman Kafka encountered who was able to see into his world and understand his writing (she was his translator); and the first to offer him her own rich world. She was not just someone 'through whom Kafka could carry on a dialogue with himself'[43] as was the case with Felice Bauer.

But this woman, this 'living fire . . . and yet most gentle, brave and wise,'[44] whom he thought he could love and perhaps have children with, was different from all the others he had met: in social standing, in her background, and in her age. Milena was married, she was Czech and she was thirteen years younger than him. Despite these barriers, their relationship flourished and after a correspondence that lasted several weeks, they met in Vienna and spent four days together, during which Kafka appeared to put his anxieties, his constant exhaustion and even his illnesses out of his mind. 'All day long he ran up and down, walked in the sun, never coughed once, ate an awful lot and slept like a log. In short, he was healthy.'[45]

He returned from Vienna enchanted and transformed. Suddenly, he was full of determination to win Milena and spend the rest of his life with her. The man who always preferred letters to personal encounters suddenly wrote: 'All writing seems worthless, as indeed it is. The best thing would probably be for me to go to Vienna and take you with me, and perhaps I shall do it, even though this is not what you want.' [46] He was prepared to elope with her, to tear her from the embrace of her husband. He began to plan encounters, this time in the German border town of Gemünd. But in letters describing the details of the rendezvous, the old fears—of intimate encounter, of 'half-an-hour in bed'—began to surface. 'Away with all this; I'm terrified of it.' [47] His anxiety grew and caused insomnia. Six weeks after their meeting in Vienna, the two met again. It was 'the most unfortunate encounter that could possibly have happened,' Milena's daughter recalled. 'The vital, impetuous, passionate Milena, and the ill, cautious and utterly passionless Kafka. Nothing happened.' [48] After the unhappy meeting in Gemünd, Kafka reverted unavoidably to his lonely state ('love is this, that you are a knife I constantly turn in my wounds'. [49]).

'You are right, too, to place what I have done now in the same category as those old things. I cannot but be always the same and live through the same. All that has changed is that I now have some experience, and I will not begin to scream until the screws are applied . . . ' [50]) The correspondence continued for a few months—letters full of fear, self-accusation, despair and depression—until Kafka broke it off. His reversion to loneliness was complete. 'I have seldom been able to cross that borderland between loneliness and sociability, seldom indeed. . . . What a beautiful, vibrant land was Robinson Crusoe's island by comparison.' [51] His last great works, 'The Burrow', 'A Hunger Artist' and, above all, *The Castle*, came out of this final period of great isolation before his death.

V

THE INITIAL SITUATION in *The Castle*, the last of Kafka's great (and unfinished) works, is the opposite of that in *The Trial*. *The Trial* opens in the morning, *The Castle* in the evening. Josef K. is taken by surprise in bed in his flat in the city. In *The Castle*, the

Land Surveyor K. comes to a strange village, looking for a bed. The lodgings he finds are miserable, only a straw mattress on the floor of a pub where the customers are still sitting; in other words, with no privacy at all. K. is a modest man, and lies down on the ticking and falls asleep. Shortly after that he is shaken awake by a young official who asks him to produce his permit to stay the night. K. is astonished. From his reply, it is clear that he has no idea where he is, yet he dismisses the young man firmly and announces that he is a land surveyor and that the count himself has invited him.

But is K. really a surveyor? After a brief misunderstanding, when the official confirms his identity, it appears that not only is the official taken aback, K. himself is surprised as well: 'So, the Castle had recognized him as the Land Surveyor. That was unpropitious for him, on the one hand, for it meant that the Castle was well informed about him, had estimated all the probable chances, and was taking up the challenge with a smile. On the other hand, however, it was quite propitious, for if his interpretation were right they had underestimated his strength, and he would have more freedom of action than he had dared to hope. And if they expected to cow him by their lofty superiority in recognizing him as Land Surveyor, they were mistaken.'[52]

The quoted passage is a typical 'Kafkaesque text', one that conceals much apparent illogicality. Why is K. overwhelmed that they recognized him as a land surveyor at the Castle? Either he is a surveyor, in which case there is no reason for him to be surprised, or he is pretending to be a surveyor, in which case why has someone in the Castle accepted and even endorsed his deception? How should the sentence: 'The Castle . . . was taking up the challenge' be interpreted? Has K. come to the village to survey or to engage in a struggle? If he has come to engage in a struggle, what is it to be about? And finally, why should the fact that they acknowledged his status as a land surveyor at the Castle indicate the 'lofty superiority' of the Castle?

Again, just as in the earlier works, there are 'illogicalities' caused by the interpenetration of two levels: the level of immediate experience, and the imagistic level into which the underlying experience has been transformed.

K. is presenting himself as someone he is not. (Here, too,

the situation is the opposite of that in *The Trial*, in which only the court believes Josef K. is someone he is not.) He never surveys anything in the village. He has no instruments. He talks about his assistants, but they never appear. He even lets slip a sentence about his wife and children, but he does so to mislead others about his identity. K. has not come to the village to survey at all, but to fight: someone is expecting K., not as a land surveyor, but as a rival, and with the spiritual advantage and the smile to which his advantage seduces him. This rival, it later appears, is an official whom Kafka named Klamm—*klam* means 'deception' in Czech. Why, however, does this castle dignitary have a spiritual advantage over K. and not, as might be expected from his position, the advantage of power? If K. thinks about the spiritual advantage of his rival, this points chiefly to the fact that the expected struggle will not be a mere power struggle, but will take place on another plane altogether. Moreover, his assumption about his rival's superiority indicates that K. already knows with whom he is in conflict.

The essential question is: what is the purpose of the surveyor's struggle? Why does he undertake the journey to this strange and gloomy place to join his battle?

The opening scene suggests the purpose of the battle K. is determined to fight. K. will fight to escape from loneliness, to gain a place among people, to prove himself capable of inclusion. It is clear what Kafka meant by that: to find the courage to live with another person, to find the strength to live with a woman, to overcome his anxiety in shared intimacy, to establish a family, to fulfil his own life and thus enter the law.

Just as the inspiration for 'In the Penal Colony' and *The Trial* came from his engagement to Felice Bauer, the impulse to write *The Castle* came from the painful experience of his failed love for Milena Jesenská, a love that was 'the strongest, the deepest and the most upsetting experience of Kafka's life.'[53]

Whereas the heroes of the first two works are merely victims who wish to escape their fates and save their own lives, the hero of *The Castle* begins his tale with the opposite intention: he wants to break out of the prison of his isolation, to become the master of his own fate, to overcome the barriers that prevent him from entering the Castle.

Just as the destiny of Josef K. is fulfilled in the course of the trial, in the vain search for proof of guilt, for the tribunal, and for a defence, so the destiny of the Land Surveyor K. is fulfilled in his vain but determined attempt to get into the Castle, or at least to speak with the powerful Klamm.

K. comes to the story with the intention of fighting for his own destiny, so there are qualities in his behaviour that are lacking in Kafka's earlier heroes. He even develops a strategy with which to approach the Castle. He dreams about how, of the two possible fates that appear to present themselves—that is, to be a village worker on the same level as the ordinary villagers, or, on the contrary, to be someone who stands outside, and perhaps above the rest, but who is completely at the mercy or the displeasure of the Castle—he will choose the lot of the worker. 'Only as a worker in the village, removed as far as possible from the sphere of the Castle, could he hope to achieve anything in the Castle itself.' He dreams of getting close to the villagers because 'then all kinds of paths would be thrown open to him.' [54] K. expects to succeed in his struggle with the castle officials, because 'well organized as they might be, all they did was to guard the distant and invisible interests of distant and invisible masters, while K. fought for something vitally near to him, for himself, and moreover, at least at the very beginning, on his own initiative, for he was the attacker.' [55]

With increasing determination, K. tries to meet with the man who can clearly decide his fate, and he dreams of his encounter with him as a moment when he will experience a feeling of freedom. ' . . . it will be sufficient for me to see what effect my words have on him, and if they have no effect or if he simply ignores them, I shall at any rate have had the satisfaction of having spoken freely to a great man.' [56] At the same time, however, he suspects that this encounter—as nothing external could—will not transform his destiny, or decide the outcome of his struggle.

In one of the most powerful scenes in the book, K. decides to wait for Klamm in the courtyard of the inn, where the sleigh is already prepared to take Klamm back to the Castle. But Klamm has no intention of meeting K. When K. refuses to obey the repeated demands by a lesser official to leave the courtyard, the driver has to unhitch the horses from the sleigh again. But K. goes on waiting. He feels 'as if the last of those people had broken off all relations with him, as if he were freer now than he had ever been, at liberty to wait in this place usually forbidden to him as long as he desired, and had won a freedom few had attained. It was as if no one could touch him or drive him away; but—and this conviction was equally strong—it was also as if there was nothing more senseless, nothing more hopeless, than this freedom, this waiting, this inviolability.' [57]

It seems, however, that the powerful Klamm, whom K. has only glimpsed through a peep-hole, is not the only one who has been informed in advance of his arrival and who has clearly decided that K. will never be received in the Castle. The barmaid Frieda also appears to have been waiting for K.: to his remark that she has only known him for half an hour, and that he hasn't been able to tell her anything about himself, Frieda replies: 'Oh, I know all about you, you're the Land Surveyor.' [58] Frieda, who until that moment had been Klamm's mistress, accepts K.'s invitation at once and, after driving the patrons out of the bar with a whip, makes love to him.

The moment K. achieves union with Frieda, his fall begins, with his vain, desperate efforts to gain control of his own destiny and to break though the blockade in which he finds himself, from the isolation of an alien experience that increasingly resembles a fatal damnation. The very act of sexual love provokes ambiguous and contradictory feelings. It does not take place in a quiet and intimate place, in a bed or even in a separate room, but on the floor of the taproom, 'among the small puddles of beer and other refuse gathered on the floor,' and when union is achieved, K. 'was haunted by the feeling that he was losing himself or wandering into a strange country, farther than ever man had wandered before, a country so strange that not even the air had anything in common with his native air, where one might die of strangeness, and yet whose enchantment was such that one could only go on and lose oneself further.' [59]

K. the outsider, who at the beginning at least gained some respect and a kind of independent position, quickly becomes an outcast in the village and eventually Frieda leaves him.

The remarkable similarities between the fate of Kafka's relationship with Milena Jesenská and the outcome of the relationship between the Land Surveyor K. and Klamm's mistress, Frieda, led the publisher Max Brod to conclude that

'In *The Castle* we find a strangely sceptical and pejorative reflection of the love relationship between Kafka and Milena . . . Milena, appearing in the novel in a highly caricatured form as "Frieda", takes decisive steps to save Kafka (K.); she unites with him, she creates a household with him in penury and self-denial, but still in joy and determination. She wants to be his for ever and in this way to bring him back to the naïvety and the immediacy of a truthful life—but as soon as K. begins to agree and takes the hand extended to him, earlier connections start to influence her ("the Castle", her humble origins, society and especially the mysterious Mr Klamm, who was based on the pompous and demonized spectre of Milena's husband, Ernst Polak, whom she never did abandon), the devoutly wished-for happiness came quickly to an end because K. is not for half-heartedness and wants to have Frieda as his wife, all to himself. . . but she betrays him, and turns back to the sphere of the Castle, from which she had come . . . '[60]

(Kafka really did attribute a kind of superiority to Polak. 'She is living fire,' he wrote to Brod, 'the kind I have never seen before, which in spite of everything burns only for him . . . But what kind of man must he be, if he can evoke that in her.'[61])

The connections that Brod makes, however, are too direct and ignore the complexities of the method by which Kafka transforms his experiences into the imagistic fabric of a story.

From what is known of Kafka and his relationship with Milena Jesenská, it is clear that he was a long way from desiring to represent that relationship pejoratively or trying to cast the blame for its rapid deterioration. His belief that he was unable to bring anything in his life to a satisfactory conclusion—and least of all his love relationships—made it a foregone conclusion that he would blame only himself for the failure of that relationship. His letters to Milena after his unhappy, fateful encounter with her in Gemünd are proof of that.

The aim of *The Castle* was not to present a negative picture of his relationship with a woman but—a return to Kafka's great theme—the fateful struggle. Kafka (in the case of Milena Jesenská) realizes (and with him his hero, the Land Surveyor K., realizes it too) that in struggling with the torture machine, with the mysterious tribunal, with the Castle, in his dilemma over marriage—the main impediments are not external enemies, nor external circumstances. The main difficulty is the hero's weakness, his inability to cross a threshold he himself has set, his inability to persuade the other 'I' to allow him to enter the place he knows is the source of an unquenchable glow.

This strange, unsettling weakness, which links K. to Josef K., is evident at the beginning of the novel, when K. still seems full of determination to fight. Abandoned by Frieda, K. continues to pursue his desperate, exhausting struggle to be received in the Castle. After several sleepless nights, he is summoned to the inn to see an official who has some news for him. But K. makes a mistake and enters the wrong door. The official, Burgel, invites him in and gradually reveals not only the secrets of the Castle's bureaucratic methods, but the secret of K.'s struggle, a struggle in which there appear 'opportunities in which, by means of a word, a glance, a sign of trust, more can be achieved than by means of lifelong exhausting efforts.' [62] From a scene in which they discuss bureaucratic methods, it changes more and more obviously into a love scene, and finally only remnants of official language shoddily disguise its essence: that it is not the lot of the weak to realize their desires. This is how the world maintains its balance.

It would seem that Brod was wrong when he compared *The Trial* with *The Castle* as parables of two leading but opposing principles: justice and mercy. *The Castle*, far more than a novel about mercy, is about a lost, squandered mercy, a lost opportunity, a defeat.

Unlike Josef K., the Land Surveyor K. voluntarily sought out his battle, and thus he knew his failing, and his guilt. How, therefore, could he remain unpunished? And truly, the punishment he gets is more cruel than the punishment meted out to

Josef K. The latter dies irradiated by flashes of a light he did not seek, but which he glimpsed. The Land Surveyor K. ends his struggle irradiated by flashes of a light he sought, but does not get to see the light.

VI

KAFKA'S MOST PERSONAL experiences—the tortured and irresolvable conflicts that filled his life—fuelled his creative impulse. But that the images of the torture machine, the omnipresent court, the mysterious trial or the Castle, are difficult to 'decipher' does not undermine their truthfulness, nor deny that they relate to basic human or social situations. On the contrary, the authenticity with which Kafka experienced his life made it possible for him to reveal the multi-dimensionality and the contradictions in his experience, all of which remained hidden from most people. Certainly, the meaning of 'In the Penal Colony' cannot be limited to a parable of Kafka's attempts to become engaged. It is merely that Kafka experienced the impending loss of freedom— an experience familiar to most bridegrooms—with an intensity that drove him to express his feelings in the terrible image of the condemned man about to be placed on the bed of a torture machine. In Felice, who was only expecting something traditional and generally accepted of him, he sensed one of the most fundamental existential contradictions. With the best will in the world, in accordance with convention, and with the general consent of society and one's own conscience, one may demand something that another will perceive as lethal. It is but a short step from this recognition to the figure of the officer—the fanatical operator of the lethal machine—to the mechanism he serves, loves, defends with conviction, and on which he is prepared to die with honour. And it is a short step to the court which, however base, corrupt, wretched and murderous, can see itself and may even be generally perceived as justified or even just.

Kafka experienced his failures in life as absolute. Whereas most people find excuses for their failures and are willing to believe they can interrupt the struggle they have entered, step out of the processes they have become involved in, cease to be lovers, husbands and wives, fathers, cease to be guilty, Kafka knew that from the moment he entered his trial or his struggle, he could not walk away from it. Nothing can be stopped; nothing, once started, can be walked away from. Once a process is begun it continues without us, without our being aware. This is a basic human situation; Kafka merely experienced it absolutely, and thus depicted it in those terms as well.

Most of Kafka's images, therefore, are presciently truthful in a general sense, not deliberately, because he had invented and constructed them to serve this purpose (as many of his imitators did) but because he was able to experience directly, deeply, unreservedly and unrelentingly the conflicts and thus the generalities inherent in every situation he entered. From this experience images were born that were so powerful and apparently so removed from their original impulse that the clarity or even the meaning of this original impulse was usually obscured.

Kafka drew these images both from traditional sources (zoology or classical mythology) and—chiefly—from the contemporary world, from his immediate experience. Thus in his writing there appear, in a mythologized form, modern offices, courts, machines, the law and, above all, a hero who carries within him not only the author's personal qualities, but also qualities characteristic of most people in the modern world; loneliness, a feeling of being at the mercy of power and of those who serve it, an insatiable longing for freedom and, at the same time, for something absolute in a world from which God has been expelled, or at least called in doubt, a longing for law and for order, a feeling of constant threat, or of alienation.

And thus a new imagistic, even mythical reality is born, one that offers many new meanings. This approach aims not merely to qualify, it may also help to assess Kafka's work in the proper spirit, not to attribute to it something it can scarcely possess: that is, an interpretation of the world. In the words of the foremost Czech literary critic, Václav Černý, 'Myth certainly illuminates reality . . . but it does not explain it, for it has nothing to do with the satisfaction of rational need and it does not try to deduce consequences in any calculable way from any causes . . . Simply put, philosophy and science are a cluster of answers to questions posed by reason. Myth and art are not a cluster of answers, but a cluster of experiences. Living is anterior to, and more fundamental than, asking and drawing conclusions.'[63]

Kafka's dogged concentration on himself, on his own experiences and on the meaning of his existence, and his extraordinary capacity to relive his conflicts on the metaphorical level, determined that he would create a work that turns our attention towards the most basic questions of our existence, from the transformations that affect the external world to the transformations of our spirit, from the processes that take place in the world to the process—or trial—that is conducted with us and with us alone, from alien verdicts to the inevitability of the verdict upon one.

At a time when the world was immersed in war fever or revolutionary fervour, when even those who thought of themselves as writers succumbed to the illusion that history was somehow greater than man and truth, and revolutionary ideas more important than human life, Kafka mapped and defended the most intimate of human space. While others thought it necessary to lay siege to heaven and set palaces alight for the welfare of humanity, Kafka was afraid man might lose his most private and final resort, the peace and quiet of his own bed.

In a world where external aims present themselves as the highest, where man appears lost in the giant shadow of his own work and of revolutionary epochs, Kafka appears as an obsessive eccentric. Compared with the grand sweep of history, the experience he offers is slight. The pictures he paints may seem small and grey compared with the colourful variety of life, and his heroes may seem too authentic in their vain efforts to get answers to the most ordinary questions and to transcend the border of the space they inhabit, at a time when man believed he had found the answer to questions of cosmic significance. But this was precisely how Kafka worked his way through to the fundamental experiences and feelings of contemporary man.

Literature that is directed outward is, for the most part, deceptive. It fixes readers' attention on external aims and thus arouses false hopes or superficial despair. There is nothing like that at all in Kafka's world; it is too inward-looking. Like someone in the real world, a person in Kafka's world leads an apparently quiet and well-ordered life until the time of his ordeal. This moment may be chosen by fate, or may be influenced by the person's own decision, but it always brings with it a clash with the world—with people who are alien. Strangers surround Karel Rossmann, the condemned man in the penal colony, Josef K. and the Land Surveyor K. They pass judgement, get in the way, send letters and memoranda, make decisions regarding life or external freedom; they are spectators to love, despair, sex. There is neither hatred nor love nor compassion in them. Life and death meet and mingle in them, just as in *The Castle* 'life and vocation [were] . . . so interlaced that sometimes one might think that they had changed places.'[64] The office, the court, the Castle are all places that embody—in harmony with experience—this sense of alienation, the unbridgeable gap that opens up between people.

Kafka's heroes move in a space in which encounters cannot take place, in which even those who are close may become enemies, and in which, therefore, a meaningful act is impossible. Like everyone who is denied the possibility of action, these heroes are at the mercy of forces that they can neither influence nor understand, and which must appear to them as hostile. Such a person lives in anxiety and doubt. He lives in uncertainty about the world around him and about the meaning of his life and in anxiety for his life. The meaning of life, its certainty, is constantly decreasing, shrinking into more and more private dimensions, until the one and only symbol of privacy left, the last space of freedom—or at least intimacy—is the bed. This is approached by uninvited, alien messengers, who are uninvolved and unaware, in order to desecrate the bed, to deprive the hero of his last refuge, to drag him out into the cold where he will be knocked about a while longer before other messengers arrive, equally alien and uninvolved, to drive a knife into his heart.

Although many have attributed the highest metaphysical aims to Kafka, his hero is, above all, a hero for our time, a godless age in which power endowed with a higher meaning has been replaced with a vacuous power of tradition and legal and bureaucratic norms, that is, by human institutions. Man, deprived of all means and all weapons in his effort to achieve freedom and order, has no hope other than the one provided by his inner space. 'At least to speak freely before a powerful man', at least to give freedom to the authenticity of his own inner being, regardless of whether the world around sees this as mere stubbornness or even stupidity. To live life authentically, to accept completely one's destiny, however difficult, regardless of whether one is marked in the end by a sentence of death, to wage a constant battle to let at least a glimmer of light into life, absolute radiance that gushes forth from the law. That, above all, is the meaning of the life—or the struggle—for the Land Surveyor K.

Just as the story of Prometheus is a myth from the heroic period of human history, the stories of Josef K. and the Land Surveyor K. are myths that belong to the present, unheroic period of human history. And just as Prometheus's act would not have been heroic without the completeness of his sacrifice and suffering, which he accepted, refusing the undignified mercy offered to him, so there would not be the unheroic stories of the condemned man on the bed of the torture machine, of Josef K. or of the Land Surveyor K., without the fullness of the sacrifice and suffering of Franz Kafka. Only someone who is willing to let himself be shackled to a rock and expose his own organs to the mercy of the eagles can offer mankind the fire to light his way through the paths of darkness.

Written for the Kafka Conference at the University of British Columbia in Vancouver, 1983.

1. Franz Kafka, *Diaries*, Vol II
2. Elias Canetti, introduction to *Letters to Felice*, Penguin
3. Franz Kafka, *Diaries*, Vol II
4. Franz Kafka, *Dopisy Milene [Letters to Milena]*, Academia, Prague, 1968
5. Franz Kafka, 'Letter to my Father', published in *Svetova literatura*, 1962, Vol VI
6. Franz Kafka, *Dopisy Milene [Letters to Milena]*, Academia, Prague, 1968
7. Franz Kafka, *Aphorisms*, Prague
8. Franz Kafka, *Description of a Struggle*, Prague, 1968
9. Franz Kafka, *Aphorisms*, Prague
10. Franz Kafka, *Letters to Felice*, Penguin
11. Franz Kafka, *Aphorisms*, Prague
12. Max Brod, *Franz Kafka*, Odeon, Prague, 1966
13. Franz Kafka, *Diaries*, Vol I, Schocken Books, New York, 1965
14. Ibid
15. Franz Kafka, *Description of a Struggle*, Prague, 1968
16. Søren Kierkegaard, *The Present [Soucastnost]*, Mlada Fronta, Prague, 1968
17. Franz Kafka, *Dopisy Milene [Letters to Milena]*, Academia, Prague, 1968
18. Ibid
19. Ibid
20. Franz Kafka, *Diaries*, Vol II
21. Ibid
22. Franz Kafka, *Letters to Felice*, Penguin
23. Heinz Politzer, *Franz Kafka*, Cornell University Press, 1962
24. Ibid
25. Max Brod, *Franz Kafka*, Odeon, Prague, 1966
26. Franz Kafka, *Dopisy Milene [Letters to Milena]*, Academia, Prague, 1968
27. Franz Kafka, *Letters to Felice*, Penguin
28. Ibid
29. Ibid
30. Franz Kafka, *Diaries*, Vol II
31. Ibid
32. Franz Kafka, *Stories*, Prague, 1964
33. Ibid
34. Ibid
35. Franz Kafka, *The Trial*
36. Franz Kafka, *Stories*, Prague, 1964
37. Ibid

[38] Ibid

[39] Franz Kafka, *The Trial*

[40] Ibid

[41] Franz Kafka, *Diaries*, Vol II

[42] Franz Kafka, *Letters to Felice*, Penguin

[43] Elias Canetti, introduction to *Letters to Felice*, Penguin

[44] Franz Kafka, from a letter to Max Brod dated May 1920, quoted in *Dopisy Milene [Letters to Milena]*, Academia, Prague, 1968

[45] Milena Jesenská to Max Brod, *Dopisy Milene [Letters to Milena]*, Academia, Prague, 1968

[46] Franz Kafka, *Dopisy Milene [Letters to Milena]*, Academia, Prague, 1968

[47] Ibid

[48] Jana Černa, *To Milena Jesenská*, Prague, 1969

[49] Franz Kafka, *Dopisy Milene [Letters to Milena]*, Academia, Prague, 1968

[50] Ibid

[51] Franz Kafka, *Diaries*, Vol II

[52] Franz Kafka, *The Castle*, translated by Willa and Edwin Muir, Secker & Warburg, London, 1965

[53] F. Kautmann, introduction to *Dopisy Milene [Letters to Milena]*, Academia, Prague, 1968

[54] Franz Kafka, *The Castle*, translated by Willa and Edwin Muir, Secker & Warburg, London, 1965

[55] Ibid

[56] Ibid

[57] Ibid

[58] Ibid

[59] Ibid

[60] Max Brod, *Franz Kafka*, Odeon, Prague, 1966

[61] Franz Kafka, from a letter to Max Brod dated May 1920, quoted in *Dopisy Milene [Letters to Milena]*, Academia, Prague, 1968

[62] Franz Kafka, *The Castle*, translated by Willa and Edwin Muir, Secker & Warburg, London, 1965

[63] Václav Černý, *Studie a eseje z moderni svetove literatury [Essays and Studies in Modern World Literature]*, Prague, 1969

[64] Franz Kafka, *The Castle*, translated by Willa and Edwin Muir, Secker & Warburg, London, 1965

ALSO BY IVAN KLÍMA AND
AVAILABLE FROM GRANTA BOOKS:

Waiting for the Dark, Waiting for the Light

'A moving and remarkable novel.' Douglas Hurd

'Although the book is about the Czech experience, it is of universal import. Klíma has some searingly truthful things to say about the wretchedness of human mediocrity, but with its hint of surrealism and its wonderful black humour, it is immensely enjoyable.' *Spectator*

The Ultimate Intimacy

'A writer of enormous power and originality.' Patrick McGrath

'*The Ultimate Intimacy* is a quiet, intense study of a man who moves from a state of emotional neutrality to one of controlled complexity . . . Klíma skilfully catches the confusion, ambiguity and the stalemate strangling of the lives of his characters . . . [his] achievement remains his understanding of moral and emotional confusion and his ability to question these dilemmas.' Eileen Battersby, *Irish Times*

My Golden Trades

'Each of the six stories here is based on a job that the narrator, a banned writer, is forced to do for economic or psychic survival . . . Klíma gives us many melodies: a real and terrifying world, a caustic and philosophic commentary, and a transcendent imagination . . . some of the best stories I've ever read.' Carole Angier, *New Statesman & Society*

'A consistent celebration of man's freedom from the tyranny of circumstance . . . Klíma has turned the various humiliating trades which he was forced to practise into the purest artistic gold.' Michael Dibdin, *Independent on Sunday*

For further information about Granta Books
and a full list of titles, please write to us at

Granta Books

2/3 HANOVER YARD

NOEL ROAD

LONDON

N1 8BE

enclosing a stamped, addressed envelope

You can visit our website at

http://www.granta.com